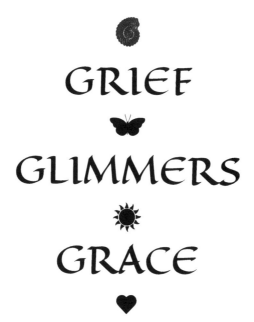

GRIEF

GLIMMERS

GRACE

CONTENTS

For the 108+ people I offered blessings for at the Ganges River on February 26, 2022.
May our collective prayers bring salvation and peace in this life and beyond.

For anyone who is hurting, may you look for the glimmers, may you rest in the grace.

This book reflects the author's present recollections of experiences over time. Some names and characteristics have been changed and some events have been compressed.

INTRODUCTION

My Living Afterlife

Sheri McKain was nine years older than me. We met in Indiana. I was starting a family and Sheri was a highly successful executive. It was an unlikely friendship because I walked away from my career in TV and radio news to immerse myself in marriage and babies and breastfeeding while Sheri was thriving in a big media career. She was breaking barriers and glass ceilings for women like me, but I chose to put it aside for a family. Sheri and her husband, Scott, moved on to LA and then Las Vegas for their careers. After a divorce in 1999, I moved to Miami Beach with my four young children. For fifteen years, we got to witness each other's worlds through birthdays, moves, promotions, separations, disappointments, and love stories.

In 2003, Sheri was diagnosed with ovarian cancer. We talked on the phone often about how she was feeling,

1

and then she wanted the gossip on my often humorous post-divorce dating. While the cancer was serious, our conversations always ended in laughter because Sheri made it possible to bring humor into challenging moments of humanity.

Between chemo and radiation and experimental treatments in Mexico, Sheri worked hard to heal, but the cancer stuck around. Without stating the truth—that we were both scared to lose her to cancer—we decided to start writing stories to each other based on writing prompts. Questions like: Tell me more about your childhood bedroom. Tell me more about your favorite time of life. Tell me more about falling in love. Tell me more about something you are proud of that not many people know about. We knew each other well, but the idea was to get to know more of each other through stories. The idea was to make the time that we had together matter even more.

Before we started writing our stories to each other, Sheri went into a surgery that was expected to extend her life. Instead, the doctors found that her cancer had spread, and she had only a short time to live. Instead of writing our stories, we spent her last weeks together in hospice. Scott stayed with her during the days, and I would stay with her during the nights.

During that time together in hospice, Sheri and I were unable to share any more stories with each other; instead, we shared the sacred time when someone is preparing to die. We spent much of that time holding hands and breathing together. I was forty-two and Sheri was fifty-one years old. She was struggling and confused about where she was because she'd gone into the hospital for surgery and woke up in hospice.

One late afternoon, just as the hot July sun was streaming through the window of her room, Sheri gave me a gift, a glimmer of the afterlife. "Daddy's in the room," she said. "Do you see him?" (Her father was dead.) I didn't see anyone, but I heard Tibetan chimes outside; it was the first time I'd heard them. "He's right there," she said, lifting and pointing her left hand.

I looked into the empty space beyond her hand, and even though I couldn't see anything, I believed her. "Yes, he's right there," I confirmed. Sheri had mostly been in a gentle coma, but now she was smiling and speaking. Her face was glowing. I stayed quiet so she could be with her dad.

After that, Sheri lived another ten days. She didn't speak again while I was with her, but that visit from her father brought her clarity and peace. Early in the morning of June 28, 2005, Sheri died as I slept next to her bed.

When I called Scott at their home to tell him, he said, "I already know. She came to me during the night." She was already starting to give us glimmers of her afterlife.

Sheri didn't leave me with any of her written stories, but she left me with the urge to write mine, and she left me the promise of an afterlife, both for her and for myself. She was in the afterlife we go to when we die; I was in an afterlife that comes when you are left behind to keep living after death has taken your friend. I was existing in the living afterlife.

I started with the writing prompts we planned on doing together, and as I wrote, I imagined I was telling the story to Sheri. Tell me more about a moment that made you cry. Tell me more about learning to swim. Tell me more about a scar that healed. Writing each story was like one of our phone calls. I always felt better after our conversations—and I always felt better after writing.

It surprised me that the memories and stories that started coming through were things I'd never shared with Sheri before. The prompts were bringing up parts of my life I'd never shared out loud with anyone. Although I'd worked in TV and radio news before my marriage, I didn't realize all the ways I'd stopped using my voice until I started writing down the stories the writing prompts inspired. Those stories became the seeds of the book *Autobiography of an Orgasm*. When it was released, I dedicated the book to Sheri. It's my story, but it also holds the unexpressed stories of so many of us who tuck away an important part of ourselves in a journal and lock it away like our voices don't matter. Writing those stories to Sheri unexpectedly helped me process, heal, and grow after trauma. Writing those stories helped me heal as I grieved. Writing those stories couldn't bring Sheri back to life, but the writing did bring me back to life. The writing offered me a living afterlife with glimmers of joy beyond the sadness.

The unexpected death of my youngest son, Charlie, in July 2022 shattered my life. I have known grief, but I've never known the kind of grieving that I continue to experience over a year after his death. I have known sadness, but I never knew the sorrow and heartache over saying goodbye to the physical body of my son.

Charlie's body was found dead from an overdose on a Friday, and the next morning I started writing and didn't stop. I wrote to record every detail of our last hug. I wrote to make sense of what happened. I wrote to remember every moment of Charlie's twenty-seven years of life. I wrote to try and understand the moment that broke him, and as I wrote, I listened so Charlie could tell me more.

As I wrote to honor and remember him, I discovered I was also writing to honor the pieces of myself that had become lost in his death: my faith, my intuition, my passion, my voice. It's like Charlie was guiding me to remember the healing spaces and sacred shrines within. "Pull over here, Momma, look at this view, let's sit awhile and remember."

Two months before Charlie died, he sent me a long letter that he'd written to himself. He wrote the words and apologies he longed to hear from others, and he wrote the words he needed to hear to heal. I'd always encouraged him to write a book, but he told me, "I don't want to write a book. I will talk to anyone who will listen. I will listen to anyone who wants to talk."

I wrote all the stories in this book during the year after Charlie died. I wrote the words I needed to hear to try and heal. I wrote as I listened to the liminal space I was existing within, and I wrote to listen to glimmers of Charlie from the afterlife. I hope that after reading these stories, you'll be nudged to write your own. I hope you write to find meaning in the unspoken stories of a grieving heart, glimmers of the promise of an afterlife, and grace in the journey.

There is no beginning or end with grief. There is the promise that it can coexist with tender moments of grace and glimmers into what's next both for our loved ones in spirit and for ourselves while we are still living. Charlie gave me many gifts during his twenty-seven years of life. After he died, Charlie taught me the gift of listening so I could continue in the living afterlife.

In the *Writing Under the Influence* section of this book, there are fifty-two weeks of writing prompts. Like Charlie, you don't need to write a book, you only need to listen to the stories and memories that want to be revealed. (I hope you write a book…). I'll be listening.

Love from Betsy

GRIEF

THE LAST HUG

J ust after Charlie turned sixteen, he told me he had a premonition that he was going to die young. Charlie was very intuitive; we all are, but many of us lose that internal compass as we grow. I appreciated that he felt comfortable sharing the information with me, and I also suggested that parts of us die during our lifetime when we let go of old wounds and old behaviors and old stories. Parts of us "die young" as we heal, evolve, and grow. Charlie nodded and said, "That makes sense." I told him that maybe he wasn't truly going to die, maybe there would come a time in his life when he would rebirth himself. He shook his head like he'd heard me and then told me again, "I believe I'm going to die young."

By the time he was a teenager, Charlie had experienced physical, emotional, and mental damage, the kind that can be buried with drinks and drugs and lies and secrets. And then he did what many do to heal—he moved as far away as possible from the people and places in Indiana that hurt him. In his early twenties, he did rebirth himself, in Northern California.

Charlie first moved to California when he was seventeen and went to Oaksterdam University to study the cannabis industry. At that time, cannabis was moving from being criminalized to being medicine, like it was always meant to be. Northern California was the site of the first Gold Rush in the 1850s, and now Charlie was seeing it happen again, this time with weed. "I just want to teach people to grow their own," he told me. "Weed is medicine; it shouldn't be treated like gold." Charlie was right, but he also saw an opportunity to make money before big companies came in and took over the industry. Within ten years, cannabis sales in just California were over $5 billion. Charlie had several big grows, but the real gold was meeting Harley and becoming a father to their girls, Sunny and Ray.

Many early cannabis entrepreneurs like Charlie paid the price, as local laws were changing rapidly during that time. More than once, local police deemed his multi-million-dollar crops illegal and burned them. Charlie watched, handcuffed, as his gold turned to ash. He moved to California to heal from early trauma only to experience more. He always rebounded with a new plan with bigger potential, but by his mid-twenties, I could see the disappointments stealing some of his joy. I could see the new wounds starting to open the old ones. I could feel it when we hugged. Every so often he'd remind me, "I believe I'm going to die young."

I remember the last hug with Charlie. It was June 25th, almost a month before he died. I'd taken him shopping for new clothes. He'd been living in a hotel for two months, away from his rural Northern California home, and he had been wearing the same thing every day— a baggy pair of dark green sweatpants, a bright blue Hawaiian shirt, and well-worn flip flops. The waistband on the sweatpants was broken, so he had tied the string in a triple knot to hold them up. Nothing matched. On any other person, the outfit would have given you the vibe that they were homeless, but Charlie wore his clothes like he was walking into a celebrity photoshoot.

Charlie always joked with his three older siblings that he was the best-looking kid in the family. He had a beautiful face with a bright smile and a nose that looked like it belonged on a Greek statue. His blue eyes reminded me of the ocean on a perfect day. When he was feeling his best, Charlie's good energy entered the room before he did. When he was at his worst, the blue nearly drained from his bloodshot eyes, and he needed to keep his distance, especially from anyone he loved. Or from anyone who was trying to love him. On the day I gave him the hug, he was starting to let me in, he was letting love in again.

Charlie was staying at a Sacramento hotel to have access to doctor's appointments. The previous year he'd been diagnosed with a cyst in his brain caused by a parasite. It was treatable, but if ignored, it could cause damage, even death. Charlie was also having other physical issues including numbness in his fingers and toes, blurry vision, and headaches. The cyst might have caused all of these symptoms, but they could also have stemmed from years of unhealthy choices like alcohol, drugs, and a mind that went to dark places when unhealed trauma kicked in. Charlie kept telling me he was going to go to Indiana because his dad was going to get him appointments with the best doctors. His dad told me that Charlie needed to stay in California where he had health insurance. Charlie was born in Indiana but had been back only once in the past ten years. I know he wanted to go there for more than doctor's appointments. He wanted connection. He wanted hugs. He wanted to be wanted.

I lived forty-five minutes from the hotel in Sacramento where Charlie was staying. On the day of the last hug, we went shopping so he could get some new clothes. In three weeks, he was turning twenty-seven, so it was early birthday shopping. He picked out every colorful

Hawaiian shirt in XXL. He preferred his shirts slightly baggy, and he always wore them unbuttoned to show off his chest hair. It was his look, especially since he liked knowing he had more chest hair than his two brothers, or his dad. He got the best hair in the family. With his shirt open and the thick dark brown hair on his head slicked back, Charlie looked like Miami meets Hollywood.

I'd gone into Target expecting to buy him a few things. He loaded up on Hawaiian shirts and then found some colorful swim trunks and baggy shorts—always his preference since he was a child. As he kept shopping, I got a cart. Charlie got new flip flops, tennis shoes, slippers, and his favorite—a blue robe. Even as a child, he loved wearing robes. He also found a pair of light gray slacks. "I can wear them with a nice shirt for my birthday dinner," he said. The only thing he didn't get was underwear. "I don't wear them," he smiled. "I like my freedom."

As we checked out, the basket was overflowing. It came to just over $750, way more than I had planned to spend, and way more than my budget. I almost asked him to put things back, but I didn't. For the first time in a long time, he was off drugs and alcohol. I felt like I had my Charlie back and it was worth every dollar I was spending. As the cashier scanned the items, Charlie chatted with her and helped to fold the clothes and put everything in bags.

"Thanks, Momma," he said. "I really appreciate everything. I'll pay you back." He always said that. "I'll pay you back." He'd seen how much I had downsized my life in the last ten years. He knew how hard I was working and how much I wanted to have a home again. "I'm going to buy you a big home, Momma," he said. "And we'll go on family vacations like we did before." His father hadn't included him on a family vacation in nine years. He had family in California—me, his girls, Sunny and Ray, and their mother, Harley, but he still wanted the family that no longer existed, the family of his childhood in Indiana.

After we left Target, Charlie asked to go to a crystal store. He wanted to buy items for clearing and protection. His body was still detoxing, and he was having bad dreams. I wanted him to stay with me, but I lived in a rental property, and I couldn't have dogs. Charlie had his dog Balto, an Australian sheepdog, with him at the hotel. It's hard to admit, but he felt safer with Balto than he did with his birth family, and Balto may have been the only 'person' who Charlie truly let love him in the last months of his life.

Trauma doesn't like to be touched. Trauma doesn't like to tell the truth. I learned that after years of pushing away people I loved because my body was constantly in a state of fight or flight, thinking I was in danger. I was safe, but the impact of the trauma lived in the memory of my cells. It was exhausting, like always being on alert and constantly running to an end that never comes. Even when I was with a trusted lover, my heart would start racing with anxiety and every fiber would contract thinking I was going to be assaulted again. I'd smile and fake it. In my forties, as I spent ten years healing, I didn't just look at the parts of me that needed to die, I also looked at the pieces of me that needed to be loved. I hoped that Charlie could get there too.

We found a spiritual shop in a rundown Sacramento strip mall not far from his hotel. "Cristales, Velas, Tarot, Espiritual" was on the sign in the window. I admired his choice to seek out protection from bad dreams using crystals and sage instead of a drink or drug. I had to take a phone call, so I handed him cash to shop while I waited in the car. "Thanks, Momma," he said as he sprang out of the car. On the drive from Target, he'd already changed into one of his new shirts, a pink Hawaiian shirt. I not only had Charlie back, but I also had a Charlie I'd never known—an almost twenty-seven-year-old Charlie who was practicing forgiveness and being curious about others' responses to his pain (or lack of response). Mostly, he wanted to get his mind and body healthy so he could spend more time with Sunny and Ray. For the first time, he was living with hopes and dreams that weren't sabotaged by trauma.

Twenty minutes later, Charlie walked out of the spiritual shop waving and smiling to the person inside. He was carrying a large bag. He opened the car door and got in. "The owner was the nicest man. He didn't speak much English, but he helped me find the right candles and crystals," he said. "He also gave me this bracelet. He said it's for protection."

We drove back to the hotel. Balto was there and needed to go for a walk. There had been so many bad moments with Charlie, especially in the past three years, that I didn't want this good one to end. But I knew I'd see him again in a few weeks for his birthday.

I pulled up to the hotel, and Charlie got out. "Thanks for everything, Momma," he said. "Love you." Instead of just saying goodbye in the car, I turned off the engine and met him on the sidewalk. The new pink shirt hung over his dark green sweatpants that should have been thrown away long ago. He smiled his movie-star smile, and his blue eyes matched the sky. It was a perfect summer day, just like July 17, 1995, the day he was born. I started to take a photo of us together, but something stopped me. I knew I would remember the feeling of that moment. It's hard to admit, but in the last two years of Charlie's life, I was aware that he might not make it. For the first time in a while, though, I had hope, and I didn't want to jinx it with a photo. Does that make sense? Not taking a photo was my protection, reassuring me that there was always a chance to take another one. Instead, we hugged. I felt his strong shoulders wrap around mine, and our hearts leaned towards each other. After a few seconds, he started to pull away.

"You have to hold a hug for at least twenty seconds for it to matter," I said. "I read that after twenty seconds, hugs become medicine." Charlie and I reached for each other, and we held onto each other for twenty seconds longer, our heartbeats in sync, just like when he was in my womb. We both needed the medicine. When it was over, he walked towards the hotel entrance, smiling, with his bags full of new clothes and crystals and candles.

I never saw him alive again. Ten days after his twenty-seventh birthday, my son was dead in his hotel room. The coroner ruled the death an accidental fentanyl poisoning, but there was enough cocaine in his body and Xanax and LSD and a half glass of red wine nearby that it didn't seem accidental to me. It seemed like he was always telling me the truth when he said he knew he would die young.

When I went to pick up his belongings from the hotel, the first thing I saw when I entered the room was an altar he'd set up with candles and spiritual books that he bought at the place we went shopping for his birthday. They were right next to the place where he took his last breath. There was a small Buddha and crystals and sage. The rest of the room was trashed, but in one area was hope and healing and that's the area where his body was found, so close to hope, so close to healing, so close to our last hug.

GETTING LOST

The day after my son Charlie was discovered dead in the hotel room, Harley and I drove there to pick up his belongings. It was a standard all-suites hotel chain, near the Sacramento airport. He'd been staying there for a month to be closer to doctor's appointments. I spoke to the manager of the hotel on the phone, and he offered his condolences and then told me to bring a mask and gloves. "We can let you in the room to get his things," he said, "but it's pretty bad."

When we arrived at the hotel, I stopped at the reception desk to get a key to the room. The young woman working there looked shocked when I explained who I was and why I was there. I was shocked hearing the words come out of my mouth. "My son died. He was staying here. I'm Charlie's mom. I'm picking up his things." The manager hadn't told her to expect me, and she also was unaware that Charlie was dead. She'd been off work for two days. "I usually work in the evenings," she said, "and

Charlie always stopped by to see if he could order some-thing for me on Door Dash. He always checked to see if I was okay or needed something to eat." She handed me a key. Then she asked us to wait for an employee to escort us to the room.

Two employees arrived and we followed them to the elevator and then up to the third floor and down a long hall to room 305. They handed Harley and me masks and gloves. We declined. One of the men unlocked the door. I exhaled, walked into the room, and inhaled as deeply as possible, hoping to catch some of Charlie's last breath. Harley was behind me, but she didn't get far. She froze against the wall closest to the door. Three weeks earlier, she had visited Charlie at the hotel. She brought him a homemade meal. The room had been clean, and he'd covered the table lights with scarfs to make the lighting softer. He'd lit a candle and asked Harley when they could have another baby. Harley smiled and said not right now. They made plans to visit again in two weeks for his birthday. They had been living apart while Charlie tried to heal from trauma that was now expressing itself through physical and mental health issues.

I'd met Harley five years earlier. It was Easter Sunday and Charlie was living in a trailer on property he was developing into a cannabis farm in Northern California.

He'd met her six months earlier, and he'd convinced her to quit college, or at least skip some classes, to help him start the farm. He hadn't told me about her, so when I arrived with a big Easter basket, I was surprised to see a young woman with long, thick, wavy dark hair emerging from the trailer they were living in. She looked like an earth mermaid wearing a long flowing dress and a gentle heart. As we walked the 200-acre property together, Charlie told me about his hopes and dreams for the land and his hopes and dreams with Harley. I left there that day knowing my son had found a partner and a love story. That summer, Charlie called to tell me he was going to be a father. Harley had just turned nineteen. Charlie had just turned twenty-one. They looked so happy. The next March, their first girl, Sunny, was born, and ten months later, their second daughter, Rayna, joined the family. After their births, Charlie bragged about "the twins," and then he slowly started to disappear into episodes of depression and manic behavior caused by years of familial trauma and unhealed pain.

Now, five years later, Harley and I enter the room where he died. The room was unsettled physically and energetically. It was trashed, like a storm had come through and lifted everything up, swirled it around, and then dropped it. It took us a moment to remember that

Balto, his Australian sheepdog, had been with him when he died, and the patches of black hair all over the floor were Balto's. There was unfinished food and bags of trash. The television was still on.

The one area that was in order was a small altar he set up on a table near the kitchen area of the small hotel suite. There was a dish with sage, crystals, and a small Buddha. There was a stack of five books. Three were about world religions and spirituality. Two were stories of recovery from drugs and alcohol abuse. I lit the sage Charlie had on his altar and walked around the room looking for notes or a message or any clues to what happened or why it happened. The only thing I found was his unhealed pain.

I'd come to take his belongings, but I chose to leave most of it in the room (something I later regretted). None of it mattered. None of it would bring him back, and all of it was touched by his death. I took the books he was reading. I took his crystals that were supposed to protect him. As we left, I picked up the remote to turn the TV off, but Harley asked me to leave it on. She was still against the wall and had barely moved. I pressed the sage into a glass to stop it burning, and we closed the door.

Ten days later, Harley and I took another drive together, this time to see Charlie's body and say goodbye.

The rest of my family remained in Indiana. Charlie's dad and two brothers chose to not come to California for the viewing. His sister Lucy was making her way home from Europe for a celebration of Charlie's life to be held in Indianapolis. Charlie had lived in California for ten years and had been back to Indiana only twice. When he died, he was planning a trip home, but the home he wanted to return to no longer existed.

After he was found, the coroner wouldn't let me see Charlie's body until an autopsy was completed. They couldn't tell me when the autopsy would be done, so I waited and waited. Harley and I both wanted to go to him right away, but we were not allowed. I needed to be with my son. His heart was created inside of my womb, and I couldn't find myself since it stopped beating. I was out of alignment and disoriented. I was missing a beat. Two days in a row I drove somewhere and got lost. People kept saying to me, "Sorry about your loss," but it wasn't Charlie who was lost. I was lost.

It was a hot Friday afternoon in Sacramento, over 105 degrees, when Harley and I drove to the viewing. I was not from the area, so I chose the funeral home based on a Yelp review. As we pulled into the industrial park that GPS directed me to, I wondered if I had the address wrong. All the buildings were a faded terracotta and looked the same. There were no signs and very few windows, only doors with numbers. As my heart sank, I realized the viewing was taking place at the same site where Charlie would be cremated. We saw a woman standing outside a door. She waved. I took a deep inhale to pull my heart back up into my chest and parked.

"Hi, I'm Kathy," she said. She held out a clipboard with papers for me to sign before we went inside. It wasn't just paperwork; it was giving her permission to cremate my son's body. My hand shook as I signed. Harley stood still next to me, holding two baskets of fresh flowers. She was only twenty-four, too young to be saying goodbye to her hopes and dreams.

After I returned the paperwork to her, Kathy said, "It took a lot of work, but he looks good now." I couldn't comprehend what she was saying or why she was saying it. I knew Charlie had been dead for at least two days before he was discovered in the hotel room. Rage rose from my core, but no words came out. Kathy opened the door. I ran to him.

I'd waited ten days to finally be with my son. I couldn't stop kissing his forehead. It was cold and I wanted to warm him up. I noticed that Kathy had parted his hair on the wrong side, but like she said, he did look good. I also looked closer to see what she needed to cover up.

I didn't want to only see him looking good, I wanted to know him in death too.

Harley and I stood next to him. The mother of his children, and me, his mother. The Mothers. There were three long rows of chairs behind us. It stung to see them empty.

He looked beautiful.

He looked at peace.

He looked like he still had more living to do.

I begged him to come back.

Harley and I both dropped into some kind of trance and began to offer prayers to him with each flower we placed in the casket. We surrounded his body with a blanket of flowers, with a blanket of love. I thanked him for trying so hard to stay alive in a world that wasn't always kind or safe for him. I thanked him for bringing the girls and Harley into my life. I thanked him for sharing so much of his life experience with me—including his pain—in the last few months of his life. I understood that in many ways, he was preparing me for his death and destiny.

Charlie's hands were crossed on top of his heart. I gently lifted a hand to tie a bracelet around his wrist and then put my hands on top of his. It reminded me of when he was four years old and I'd walk him into school and say, "Give me my favorite hand," and he'd give me one of his tiny hands. And then I'd say, "Give me my other favorite hand," and he'd give me his other hand, and I'd hold both of them tight. I did that because Charlie was always running ahead to see what was next, and I wanted to keep him close to me, to keep him safe. Now as I held his hands, I blessed him for what's beyond and then I kissed him and let go.

KICKING TOWARDS
THE LIGHT

My youngest son, Charlie, learned to swim at the same time he was learning to walk. He loved the water. He had three older siblings who loved to swim, too, so Charlie often followed them into the deep end when other toddlers were still in the baby pool.

The summer Charlie turned one, he followed his brother Willie to the diving board at the country club pool. It was a sunny day in July. I was treading water in the deep end, waiting to see what Charlie would do once he reached the end of the long board. The lifeguard looked over, concerned. When his tiny toes reached the edge, Charlie stopped. He looked around to make sure his big brother was watching. With four feet of a perfect summer day between us, I said, "Charlie, if you jump, if you need me, I'll be here to catch you," and within a breath, he launched himself into the sky, smiling as his tiny body arced towards the pool. As he floated through the air, I used my hands to propel myself backward so he didn't land on me. He dropped below the surface, and I ducked underwater and watched him sink. Just when I thought I needed to reach for him, he turned towards the sun and kicked. We broke the surface together.

Everyone cheered.

I loved that he intuitively knew to turn his head and heart towards the light.

Over twenty years later, Charlie's daughters Sunny and Ray learned to swim in the pool at my home in Northern California. The previous summer, I had needed to be next to them when they swam, but last summer, they were both going off the diving board and swimming the length of the pool on their own. Sunny was five and Ray was four. It was the summer of their biggest jumps and longest swims. It was also the summer their dad died. He was twenty-seven.

A few weeks after Charlie died, Sunny intentionally started yelling for help in the pool. She swam to the deep end and then looked right at me and called for help. I said to her, "Sunny, I'm right here, but you can save yourself. You know how to swim." She flailed and dunked her head back under water. When she resurfaced, she reached one arm towards the sky for added drama and yelled, "Help me!"

Without moving to her, I said, "You can save yourself, Sunny. You can swim to the wall. Or if you are tired, you can roll on your back. I'm here if you need me, but you can save yourself."

She dunked herself under a few more times. I slowly moved a little closer. "I'm right here, Sunny, but you can save yourself. You know how to swim." Finally, she smiled and swam to me. She saved herself.

When Charlie died, I received messages from all over the world. There's a collective ache in the messages, like we all feel like we are drowning in sorrow for Charlie or for someone we love or for ourselves. We need someone to save us, to throw us a life raft. I even wanted someone to save me from this heartache and pain, and then I remembered I can save myself. We can save ourselves. We can reach for the wall or a person or roll over and float for a while until we get our strength back. I know how to do this. You know how to do this. In the last moments of his life, I wish Charlie had remembered how to do this. We must remember to reach our head and heart towards the light and kick.

MORE THAN A
STATISTIC

My youngest son, Charlie, had been twenty-seven for only two weeks when his body was found dead in a Sacramento hotel room in July 2022. He died from fentanyl poisoning. Charlie always told me he was too smart to do a bad drug.

I asked the Sacramento Police Department for help in getting my son's phone unlocked and for access to the video cameras at the entrance of the hotel. Maybe we'd find answers to who was with Charlie or who gave him the drugs. They told me they were too busy with other cases, but if I found anything, they would reopen his case. To them, Charlie was just another one of the 300 daily opioid-related overdoses in the US. To law enforcement, he was just a statistic. But to me, he was a son. To Harley, he was a soulmate and the father of their children, Sunny and Ray. To his siblings, he was a brother. He was so much more than his last choice.

When people ask me what he died from, telling them it was an overdose doesn't feel like the truth, because parts of Charlie started dying a long time ago of disappointment, disillusionment, and betrayal. If you've experienced physical, emotional, and mental trauma like Charlie did, it makes it harder to recover, so you reach for a drug or a bottle. A drug like Naloxone could have saved Charlie if someone had found him in time, but what can we do for our loved ones to save them long before they choose to take a drug that could end their lives? We can't afford to keep losing loved ones. We can afford to learn and listen.

Everyone experiences trauma, but not everyone has the resilience or support they need to recover from it. As a teenager, Charlie first found relief in weed and alcohol. He was also prescribed Adderall to help him focus in school. I fought against giving him any medication, but eventually he asked to take it. He called it his legal drug. But those weren't his gateway drugs. The gateway was the impact of our divorce early in his childhood. The gateway was when the soul of the family was broken. The gateway was abuse against his body and the silence that came after. The gateway was a traumatic brain injury when he was sixteen. The gateway was all the things we don't encourage our children to talk about, so they bring a drug to their lips instead of the truth.

At his lowest moments, Charlie's unhealed trauma turned into a mental health crisis that spun out of control and pushed away friends and family. He couldn't help himself—fight or flight is a natural response to trauma. In ten years and through some very dark moments, Charlie used drugs to bring his body and spirit back into balance. When no one wanted to listen, he saved himself over and over again. The drugs that we urged him to quit were the same ones easing his pain and keeping him alive in a world that didn't always feel safe.

I'm hanging on. I am praying. I just need a hug and I need you to listen to me about what makes me feel like I have to escape the pain. I need you to hear my stories of abuse. I need you to know I got taken advantage of and beaten and broken. I'm still here.

— **Charlie Griswold,** 77 days before he died

In the last few months of his life, Charlie wrote and spoke to me often about what happened to him that caused him to disconnect. He was trying so hard to free himself from the pain, to live in the present, and to plan for the future. A future with his young daughters. A future with family. A future helping others recover from pain similar to that which he was trying to break free from. There were also concerns about his choice to heal alone in a hotel room; animals can retreat and lick their wounds until they are better. Humans need connection. We heal in community. Too many people close to Charlie gave up on him long before he gave up on himself.

The problem was not Charlie. The problem was that we are not a trauma-informed society, we are not trauma-informed families. As he was growing up, people constantly told me what was wrong with Charlie. No one ever asked me what happened to him. More importantly, from a young age, Charlie was told what was wrong with him. No one asked him what happened. We blame the person instead of looking at what may have caused their pain or behavior. We ignore the parts of them that need attention.

Gemini Adams, a trauma recovery specialist, told me, "There is so much misunderstanding, particularly in the recovery community. Healing this kind of relational trauma, particularly from abuse, is a very specialist area and requires a multi-disciplinary approach that works with the unprocessed shame, lack of safety, and anxiety with people. It is focused on repair and trust building, not on taking the substance away from the addict as if that will miraculously stop them in their tracks. In fact, it usually has the opposite effect as it activates all the protector parts and puts them into survival mode and triggers the underlying agony they are trying to escape from, which increases the chances of suicide or a relapse that results in overdose."

Hurt people hurt people, and during the last few years of his life, Charlie was in deep pain and pushing away people he loved. But even at his lowest, he was showing up for other young adults like himself who may have been estranged from family members who were unwilling to understand their pain. Charlie helped them by listening and offering encouragement and support. It's easy to give them a label and step away. I never saw my son as an addict; I saw him as someone healing from some really hard things. Have you ever tried to heal from something hard alone?

As a trauma recovery specialist, Gemini Adams sits with many in pain. "If you can bring the pain forth of anyone, whether they are in your family or otherwise, it will be time well spent. The weight of our pain unseen, unheard, or unresolved, is by far the greatest burden we will ever carry."

We all need connection. It's easy on the good days— the challenge is to stay present with ourselves and loved ones on the hard days. Charlie needed us to show up for tough conversations and then get back to love. He needed a hug. He needed kindness. He needed to remember that he mattered, even when he was at his worst, because he was so much more than that final moment.

MY CAR,
MICHELLE

The week before my son Charlie died, I purchased a new (used) car. My current car had over 80,000 miles on the odometer, and my mechanic told me that he tends to see issues with those cars (Infinitis) after 80,000 miles. I loved my car. I thought about who I'd most want to do a road trip with, and the answer was Michelle Obama, so my ocean-blue Infiniti station wagon was christened Michelle. I really didn't want to part with her, so I searched and found the exact same car with fewer miles. I live in California, but I arranged to pick up the car at a dealership in Indiana where I would be for the month of August to support my mother through shoulder surgery. I figured I could sell Michelle in California, fly to Indiana, and then at the end of my time there, I would do a late-summer road trip back home to California in Michelle #2. I had it all planned. And then on July 29th, I found out that Charlie had died alone in a Sacramento hotel. Suddenly, all the pages of my calendar were filled with a different to-do list.

We had a small ceremony for Charlie in California and then hosted a celebration of his life the following week in Indianapolis, where he had been born. As I was organizing transportation for our time in Indianapolis, I realized I didn't need to rent a car; I could just pick up my new one.

So, we flew to Indiana, and the next morning I went to the dealership where Michelle was waiting for me. Everything I'd been doing up to that point had been around death; the lights were low in the spaces where I'd been hiding from normal life. Walking into the car salesroom was shocking. The lighting was so bright, and everyone was so friendly. I smiled and tried to fit in, to act like everything was okay. I didn't tell them why I was in Indiana.

The paperwork was over quickly, thank goodness, because I was barely holding on to the tears that needed to flow. Grief hits you anytime, anywhere…even when you are buying a car. Jenny, the salesperson, handed me the keys and eagerly walked me to my new car. It had an enormous yellow bow on the hood. Another person had a camera ready to take my photo even as I was disappearing into a cloud of sadness. Everyone congratulated me. I didn't smile, I couldn't smile. I put on sunglasses to cover the tears, got in the car, and drove away.

It was oddly comforting to have Michelle #2 to drive during the week. She wasn't a rental car; she was something familiar, but after the celebration of life for Charlie, I was not in a good emotional space to drive 2,000 miles, so I left her in Indiana, parked at my son Willie's house. I flew back to California, where Michelle #1 was waiting for me.

I hardly drove during the next few weeks. Even thinking about going to a grocery store overwhelmed me. The shock and sadness of grief kept me home. I'd cancelled all my work indefinitely. I had no income, but now I was making payments on two cars. It wasn't financially smart to continue paying for both, so I booked my flight back to Indiana to pick up Michelle #2, knowing that when I returned to California, I could sell the original Michelle.

From Indiana, the road trip back to California was oddly therapeutic. When I did stop for gas or to spend the night at a hotel, it was good to be invisible. No one knew me. No one knew I was a mother in grief, and Michelle #2 was a good companion. We listened mostly to a playlist that Charlie's siblings and Harley, the mother of his two children, Sunny and Ray, had put together. For three days, I drove west, singing through the tears, until Michelle #2 and I arrived home. Now I had both Michelles in my driveway, looking like twins reunited.

Even though the cars were the same (year, color, and model, just fewer miles on one), I found I suddenly had this odd connection to the original Michelle. Now I didn't want to sell Michelle #1 because she was the car that Charlie and I took our last drives together in. We had our final in-person conversations in that car. That car held our laughter, and it also held some painful truths that he shared with me before he died. She was also the car that held his ashes after I picked them up from the funeral home. I looked at selling Michelle #2 instead, but it would mean losing thousands of dollars on the sale, so I did what many do when pressured in grief: I put it off for a month, and then another month.

Both cars stayed in my driveway for six months. I was still making two payments for cars that I was rarely driving. Several times I had to pay to have the batteries jumped on both cars because I hardly drove at all in the months after Charlie died. I felt paralyzed in grief. I also knew I needed to sell a car. None of this was sustainable.

The temporary Indiana tag on Michelle #2 needed to be replaced with a California tag. I let it expire. I could barely handle going to the grocery store, picking up only three or four items at a time. I had to be quick because I never knew when the tears would come, and in those early months, they came all the time. And then one day, I shared with my friend Jen that I'd hardly left the house because I feared losing it, sobbing in public. I never knew when the waves of tears would rush over me. Jen's son died four months before Charlie, and she offered some valuable insight. "Just out yourself when you are in public," she told me. "Let them know that you are dealing with death and grief." I held that thought when I went to the DMV a month later to finally register the new car. I went early to try and be first in line so it wouldn't take too long. I took a number and sat down until it was called. I felt okay as I sat in the waiting area. *I can do this*, I thought. Just then, I heard my number, and I approached the window and handed the woman behind it my paperwork. She didn't look up as she accepted it. She shuffled through the paperwork, and without making eye contact, she said, "You were supposed to register this within thirty days."

I thought about reaching for the paperwork, taking it from her hands and leaving. Instead, I remembered what Jen told me. I took a deep breath to stay calm, to keep the wave from hitting me, but it was too late. I put my sunglasses on to cover the emerging tears and fanned my face with my hand, hoping to stop the flow.

"My son died recently," I said. "I've been having a hard time leaving the house. I want to finish the transaction, but I may cry. I never know when the grief will hit."

For the first time since we'd started the transaction, she looked at me. Then she reached for me, placing her hand on the counter without touching me, and she said, "I'm so sorry. That must be hard. Thanks for telling me."

It was a huge relief. I'd let someone in on my secret. Just her seeing me allowed me to stay present. I tilted my head back and opened my heart and let grace into the moment of pain, and we finished the transaction. Within minutes, she handed me my new California plates for Michelle #2 and then said, "It's okay to not be okay right now."

People often complain about the DMV, but that day, I had nothing but praise. I learned that living under the influence of death while coexisting in a world that isn't grieving with you is tricky, but if you let someone in, if you share your truth, you make space for kindness and goodness and grace.

A few weeks later, I finally said goodbye to the original Michelle. I blessed her for holding the last conversations and road trips with Charlie, knowing that Michelle #2 will hold new conversations and new road trips with his children, Sunny and Ray.

GLIMMERS

PHANTOM LIMB

P eople who lose a part of their body (leg, arm, breast...) report that they can often still feel the sensation of it being there even though it's gone. It's called phantom limb syndrome, and for me it's what the death of my son Charlie feels like. There is a sensation that he's still here, and there is also pain when I realize over and over again that he is gone. It's like a part of me is always searching for what is missing.

Charlie's death dropped me into a maze of lost hopes and dreams for my son, for his daughters, for our family, for myself. I've experienced much death in my life and have been a death doula for others, but nothing prepared me for the experience of losing a child.

The first time I read Elizabeth Kübler-Ross's book *On Death and Dying*, I was a freshman in high school, and it really stuck with me. I studied the stages of death so I would know what to expect when someone dies: denial, anger, bargaining, depression, acceptance. I worked through the steps at the tragic death of a friend when I was a teenager and then the unexpected death of my father in my twenties. In my thirties, I experienced the death of both my godfather and godmother, and once again I relied on the book to guide me from denial to acceptance. In my forties, I cared for my best friend, Sheri, during her final days in hospice. We spent her fifty-first birthday together at her home in Las Vegas. We never imagined that two months later she'd lose her battle with ovarian cancer, but Sheri and I experienced some magical moments together during her final days in hospice. Those moments allowed me to let go, accept, and be grateful that she was a part of my life and that she allowed me to be a part of her death. In my fifties, I held my stepfather, John's, hand as he took his final breaths with my mother, Virginia, cuddled next to him. John was eighty-two and lived a full life, but it's still hard to let go of someone you love.

With each death, the stages came in different order but always ended with the last one, acceptance. I worked those stages like I was running a relay, passing the baton off from one stage to the next and high-fiving myself for staying in the race. I was good at grief—until my son died.

Charlie was twenty-seven when he died; it was six months before my sixtieth birthday. It's unnatural for a child to die before a parent. I kept waking up thinking, *This isn't supposed to happen, this doesn't make sense, this must be a mistake.*

Grief makes your brain foggy, shock sends you into survival mode, sadness kidnaps your heart, and rage takes you down paths that make it hard to find your way home again. When Charlie died, I plunged into a fury that kept people from getting too close and a shock that stripped me of my life force. I felt like my heart was getting electrocuted every time I remembered he was gone. *Zap. Zap. Zap.* The grief stung over and over again.

When my rage about Charlie's death was triggered—and that was constant in the first year—the pain of the phantom limb throbbed like an ache that no medicine could heal. Survival didn't seem possible. In some ways my body sensed that it needed to die to put the order back into life. It was not fair for me to outlive Charlie.

Every day was like being in a life raft that got ripped to pieces in rapids. I treaded water to survive. The grief was exhausting. *Zap. Zap. Zap.* I wrote about my grief on social networking and found that I wasn't alone. I joined a group of 25,000 parents whose children died. I was pissed to be there, and I was also looking for answers. I was hoping to find that it gets easier. No one said it gets easier. One mother wrote to me, "I've learned that it's possible to live with a hole in your heart."

Two months before Charlie's death, he sent me a long letter. This was unusual for Charlie because he usually communicated in shorter texts and voicemails. He'd been on a healing path, and I always encouraged him to write a book and share his story. He wrote:

Alcohol is my biggest vice but I take breaks constantly. I only abuse it when I am sad and hurting and feel nobody listens. I have to be here in this life to deal with my karma. I've tried shortcuts, easy ways out. It doesn't work like that. I will create something special and good and meaningful one day. I will be loved and appreciated for who I am. I will help people and let them know you can get past this trauma.

I'm not going to write a book, I'm not going to tell the world. I will talk to anyone who will listen. I will listen to anyone who wants to talk.

Months after he died, I reread the letter and found the missing limb. To be with Charlie again, I needed to listen. I had to abandon the rage and just listen. I started writing to listen and to remember. I wanted to remember our last day together, our last conversation, our last hug. I wanted to remember how his ocean-blue eyes made feel-good waves when he entered a room. I wanted to remember his bloodshot eyes on the days that life felt too hard for him. I wanted to remember it all because those were all parts of Charlie. The good days, the hard days, and the spaces in between made up the essence of Charlie.

I started writing to keep Charlie alive, and over the next few months, I found that the daily writing was keeping me alive and guiding me through grief as a sacred pathway. Each page tended to the wounds of sorrow; the words became balm for tender inner scars to heal. Writing was like a spirit guide showing me where to look and pointing me in directions I might have missed. Often the writing was like a trance. In the same way many cultures know to dance to connect to spirit, the writing was my dance. It was filling in the hole. It was helping me to re-grow the limb.

Writing the stories supported my grief and allowed me to record the glimmers of the afterlife I was experiencing through Charlie. Charlie always believed in angels, more than I did, so when he died, I wanted to believe in them too. I wanted to believe that Charlie had joined angel school and was hanging with his favorites that he used to tell me about—Gabriel, Ezekiel, and Raphael. Most likely he was making good trouble, but most importantly he was talking to anyone who wanted to listen and listening to anyone who wanted to talk.

THE SPACE BETWEEN

I'm not new to grief. I've experienced much death in my life. I am new, though, to witnessing how children process grief. Ray and Sunny were four and five years old when their dad died, and they seem so much more resilient than me. They continue to balance moments of sadness with playing, creating art, and singing. They don't let their grief stop them from living, and that's something I need to remember right now.

My grief is slow and uncomfortable. The days and weeks and months after my son died were long and painful. My friend and teacher Laura Day always reminds us to pay attention to what we do when we are upset, sad, worried, angry, and disconnected. What do you do when you don't want to stay present with the moment? Do you medicate the pain? Do you bring a drink to your lips instead of the truth? Do you numb out to Netflix instead of being present to your own life? Do you swallow the truth instead of speaking it?

I stayed in bed. I used my covers as a cocoon and hoped that I could turn to mush and then eventually emerge as a butterfly and fly away from the pain. But really all I was doing under those covers was not staying present. I was stuck in the past. I was stuck in grief.

For the first few months after Charlie died, when the girls were over for a playdate, Sunny would stop in the middle of her playing and ask, "Is Daddy alive?"

"No," I said, unsure if I should add anything else.

"Is Daddy dead?" she continued.

"Yes, Daddy is dead."

That sentence was so hard to say. I never got used to it even though Sunny asked me every few weeks, so I had to say those words often: "Daddy is dead."

Usually, Sunny would go right back to what she was playing or drawing, but one time, she broke down and screamed until she had me crying too. Her little sister, Ray, looked at both of us and said, "Take a breath." Ray slowly raised her hands towards the sky as she said, "Inhale…" And then she slowly lowered her hands to the ground as she said, "Exhale." And then she did it again. "Take another breath. Inhale. Exhale." Sunny and I both took deep breaths into our tears and eventually stopped crying. My four-year-old granddaughter became the teacher. My breath became the medicine.

About six months before Charlie died, when we didn't know what else to do for him as he tried to heal from complex trauma, Harley and I started making offerings for him at a river near our homes. We'd hike down to the river with the girls and find rocks and blow our prayers and wishes for Charlie into the rocks.

"I pray for Charlie to heal. I pray that he knows he is loved and supported. I pray for him to remember his life path and know his value and purpose. I pray for him to get beyond the pain."

We'd have the girls blow on the rocks too—and then we'd offer them to the river. By the time he died, I'm sure the rocks and prayers we offered had created a new path in the river.

Charlie was cremated, and although we never talked about his wishes, I believe he would want his ashes spread everywhere like he was omnipresent. Harley and I decided to first take some of his ashes to that same river spot. I'd been ready to release the ashes—and not wanting to let them go. We didn't tell the girls what we were doing. The plan was a hike and swim at the river with the girls. Then Harley and I would quietly offer some of his ashes.

On the drive to the river with the ashes tucked in a bag on my lap, out of the blue, Ray asked me to tell stories about her daddy. So, I told a funny story about when we were on a flight to Florida when Charlie was six, and he ate multicolored candy, drank a Sprite, and then got sick and vomited a rainbow. The girls laughed.

"Too much candy will make you sick," I said to them as Sunny unwrapped some sweet tarts.

Then Ray asked me why her daddy died. I wasn't ready for that one. "Because his heart...stopped working," I said. "All our hearts will eventually stop working. We are all born, and we will all die." I'm looking at Harley, trying to think of a way to turn the conversation around, and I'm pretty sure I'm saying everything wrong. I didn't want to scare them but I also didn't want to bypass a question they asked. They wanted answers. "Our hearts are strong, but daddy's heart got sick," I said. Sunny stopped putting the candy in her mouth. I'm sure she was thinking about all the times we'd told her to not eat too much candy, or she'd get sick.

We parked and started hiking down to the river, and Sunny slowly dropped her sweet tarts one by one on the trail. The closer we got to the river, the more upset she got, but she couldn't tell us why. I'm sure my story in the car didn't help.

We blew bubbles, chased butterflies, and then swam and climbed on the rocks. The girls helped me offer flower petals to the river as I silently said prayers for their dad. And then, quietly, Harley offered the ashes. The girls didn't know what was happening; as the ashes swirled into the water and floated away, Sunny stopped crying. We all felt something shift. Then Ray said, "I don't want to die, I want to be alive," and she started making bubbles so "Daddy can see them in heaven."

Sunny and Ray are certainly some of my best teachers and therapists right now. One moment we can be playing a game where they wave magic wands and turn me into a frog or a fairy, and then minutes later, they will ask about their daddy and heaven, and why did he have to die? I'm always looking for new answers, to not get stuck in the old stories. They aren't always looking for a happy ending, but they are asking for the truth.

One night six months after Charlie died, the girls spent the night with me. After Ray fell asleep, Sunny got really close to me in bed and whispered, "Do you want to talk about Daddy…yes or no?"

"Yes," I whispered into the darkness. Then she started telling me a story.

"After Daddy died," she said, "his heart didn't beat anymore, and instead his heart was planted as a seed, and it started growing plants, and all the plants were blooming flowers and turning into more plants."

It felt like she was talking about the love that remains even after someone dies. It felt like she was taking a sad story and making it better—not happy, just better. My tears started rising and Sunny whispered, "Why are you crying?" even though she couldn't see me in the dark room.

"I'm crying because I'm sad that Charlie (Daddy) is dead."

"He's alive!" she said. "He's alive in heaven. He's alive in heaven."

She said it twice, like I needed to really hear it and believe it. It was something Sunny had never said before, and we've never suggested it. She was so convincing. We both fell asleep smiling. We both fell asleep believing.

Sunny likes to draw and often during the past year, she'll suddenly stop what she was doing and draw a picture of Charlie smiling and floating in the sky near the sun, like she'd just received an angel text from him. She always hands the drawings to me like they are messages and then goes right back to what she was previously drawing— a unicorn, a fairy, or vines of flowers growing from a heart. These days without Charlie are hard ones. And these days with Sunny and Ray are special ones. And I'm living in the space in between.

DO YOU NEED
A BAG?

I'm finally on the way to pick up my son's ashes. It's been three weeks since he was cremated. I didn't want to leave him alone this long. Maybe I've avoided it because I don't want it to be real. Plus, my friend Elizabeth says we are statistically at risk to get in an accident after the death of a loved one. I get it. I don't remember the drive to the coroner's office. And I don't remember the drive home from the Sacramento hotel where he died.

I do remember waking up early that day; it was before I got the call that Charlie was dead. I sat on my porch and wrote just like I always did, letting the morning sun warm me. My grandchildren were coming over to play in a few hours. It was the start of another perfect summer day.

I do remember getting the call and collapsing in shock. I was home alone, and I screamed as the rage tore through every cell of my body.

I do remember holding Harley close as I whispered in her ear that Charlie died. Charlie and Harley shared two children but no longer lived together. I held her tight as their children—my grandchildren—Sunny and Ray, were playing in her backyard. And then something odd happened. Even though Sunny couldn't hear what I said, she grabbed a flower off a tree and ran up to us, gave it to her mother, and said, "It's okay to say goodbye. Everything is okay." She said it twice, like we needed to really hear it, and then she ran off to play again.

After the day Charlie died, the weather changed. There was an unexpected rain, and then it got hot, really hot. Today, it's over 100 degrees in Northern California, and I have a forty-minute drive to the funeral home. The last place I want to be is in a car, but tomorrow I fly to Indiana to take some of his ashes to his father, so I have to go today.

I'm not familiar with the funeral home. If I were in Indiana, where I'm from, I'd know who to call. I've lived in California for only five years. I moved here to be close to Charlie and my granddaughters. I hardly know anyone in my new community, so I chose the funeral home based on a Yelp review.

Simple Blessings is in a strip mall, next to a Five Guys restaurant. Charlie would love that. Whenever he got in trouble, I'd go to pick him up, and he'd ask to go to Five Guys. First it was from the grade school counselor's office, then a middle school principal's office, or from high school detention. Later, I'd pick him up from rehabs. Once it was jail during a spring break in Panama, Florida. Every time I picked him up, he ran to the car, waving and smiling. "Thanks for picking me up, Momma" like he'd just been on some big adventure. He'd get in the car and turn up the volume on the music. I didn't like it loud, so I'd turn it back down. Then he'd ask to go to Five Guys to get a cheeseburger, fries, and a milkshake. I don't like fast food, so I never ate anything, but Five Guys was our spot to let Charlie know he was still loved and valued even on his worst days. Over a meal, Charlie would tell me his hopes and dreams, and he was so excited about his plans, it always made me forget that he was supposed to be in trouble. He was great at that, talking his way out of trouble. It was hard to be mad at him. He was the baby of the family. Charlie had three older siblings, my children Sam, Lucy, and Willie. After my divorce, his dad had three more children with two more women. Charlie went from being the youngest to being in between and in the middle of so much more than just his seven siblings. After our time at Five Guys, Charlie would always say, "It's you and me against the world, Momma."

I park between the funeral home and Five Guys. It's so hot that I sweat walking towards the door, but as soon as I enter the reception area, I immediately get chills—their AC is cranked way up. Before I see a person, I notice pale blue packages wrapped like gifts on the front desk. I look closer at the attached card. *Charles Griswold.* My six-foot-tall Charlie is now divided into five eco-friendly packages, the size of small shirt boxes.

This is all that's left of my son?

"Hey, Betsy, good to see you again. Do you need a bag?"

Do I need a bag? It's Katie, who works there. The last time I saw her was when I dropped off clothes for Charlie to be cremated in—a pink Hawaiian shirt and light gray slacks. It's Friday and Katie is dressed like she's going to a music festival. Shouldn't she be wearing black instead of tie-dye at a funeral home? And that's all she has to say to me, do I need a bag?

"No. Thanks," I say. "I brought a basket."

The basket is lined with Charlie's baby blanket. I carefully start putting the packages of ashes on top of the blanket.

"Any fun plans for the weekend?"

My son is dead. I'm not going to have a fun weekend. And please don't tell me that he's in a better place now, this too shall pass, or everything happens for a reason. And I'm stunned at the number of people who ask how he died. Why would you ever ask that? Ask me how he lived, ask me what brought him joy. And please don't ever tell me to just focus on gratitude. You know what Katie? Fuck gratitude.

I don't say any of this to her, but people have said some really harmful things since Charlie died. It's not okay. It hurts.

I head for the exit with the basket and walk back out into the heatwave. As the door shuts behind me, I hear Katie say, "Have a good day!" and my body flushes with rage.

The ashes are heavy. I use two hands to carry him just like I did when he was a baby in a car seat. I open the passenger door and carefully put the basket of what is left of my son in the passenger seat. The color of the package of ashes reminds me of Charlie's blue eyes. On his best days, his eyes sparkled like the ocean on a calm day. On his hard days, his eyes were bloodshot with fiery red veins and unhealed trauma. I wish I could have one more day with him.

I close the door and walk around to the driver's side, get in, and turn on the car. The passenger seatbelt light starts beeping, like there is someone in the seat. I reach over and buckle Charlie in, just like I had when he was a child. I pull his baby blanket over the ashes, and we start the drive home.

The last time Charlie sat in the front seat of my car was less than two months ago. We did early birthday shopping for him. We laughed at family stories. We talked about the future with his girls. He wanted to take them to Disneyland at Christmas. At the end of our time together, I dropped him off at the airport hotel where he was staying, and we gave each other a hug. I'll never forget it because, for some reason on that day, when he released the hug, I asked him to hug twenty seconds longer. I told him when you hug for at least twenty seconds, the hug becomes medicine, so he reached for me, and we held on longer as we counted to twenty. And then we let go. During those next weeks, we had several conversations, but I never saw him alive again. In a moment of pain, he chose to chill out with what he thought was Xanax and cocaine, but it ended up being cut with fentanyl. Now he's back in the front seat, buckled in, a basket filled with ashes.

Charlie always liked a good road trip playlist, and after he died, I started one with his siblings and Harley. It's filled with his favorite songs and songs that remind us of him. We played it in the background at his celebration of life. I look at the seat full of what is left of Charlie and decide to put on his playlist. I press shuffle and turn up the volume.

It's an odd thing to drive alone with your son's ashes. I try to act normal with thoughts that aren't normal. *Why won't anyone help me get his phone unlocked so we can get answers on who gave him the drugs? Why didn't I wait to cremate him so I could spend more time with his body? There's a grocery store; I have no food at home. Why didn't anyone listen to me when I raised concerns for his well-being in the few days before he died? Why was his phone turned off so soon after he died? I wish I had taken a photo of how beautiful he looked before he was cremated. I need groceries, but I don't want to leave the ashes in a hot car. I don't want to leave him alone.*

The plan is to drive home and drop the ashes and then drive another fifteen minutes back to the grocery store. I almost past the exit for Trader Joe's but at the last second, I swerve and take it. I pull into the parking lot and park. I look at the ashes, unroll the window a few inches so there is a fresh air supply, and then turn off the car. *I just need a few things, I'll be just a few minutes*, I say to no one.

I charge through Trader Joe's and quickly get my things. I'm ready to pay, but the lines are long. I stand, juggling my groceries in my arms, trying to choose the right line, the quickest line, when suddenly a young cashier waves to me and opens a new line. Another employee is there to help her bag.

"Heyyyy, how is your day going?" the cashier says.

"Uhhhh, could be better." I forgot Trader Joe's employees are friendly and very chatty. I don't want to talk to anyone.

"Well, I'm here to listen." She smiles and scans my yogurt. I fake-smile back.

"Ma'am, you can tell me anything."

She says this like she's begging me to share. Plus, I don't like being called ma'am. "You want to know how my day is going? I just picked up my son's ashes. He died. He was twenty-seven. The ashes are in my car right now. And I just need a few groceries, but I didn't want to leave him alone in the car because the last time I left him alone—"

The cashier drops the yogurt and runs off, and now I'm left there with the other employee. She drops her head and says, "I had to put my dog down yesterday."

"I'm…sorry," I say. "What was your dog's name?"

"Lucy." She smiles when she says the name, and I do too.

"My daughter's name is Lucy. My son, the ashes in the car, has a sister named Lucy. That must have been hard for you, putting your dog down yesterday and having to come into work today."

She nods and looks up with tears in her eyes. "Yes, it's been a really, really tough day."

She looks relieved that she doesn't have to fake it anymore. And now the cashier reappears with a bundle of flowers. "These are for you…from all of us," and she waves a hand across the entire store. Someone rings that damn Trader Joe's bell, and everyone cheers.

"Do you need a bag?" she says as she scans the rest of my groceries.

I take the flowers. *Do I need a bag?*

"No, I'm good. I'll be okay. Thank you."

We complete the rest of the transaction in silence. I walk back to my car, put the groceries in the back seat, and put the flowers next to Charlie, on his baby blanket in the front seat. I can almost hear him laughing at me and saying, "Well, that went well…" and then adding, "I knew this was a tough day for you, and I wanted to get you flowers."

I turn on the car, press shuffle on Charlie's playlist, turn up the volume, and we finish the road trip home.

BELONGING

It's my third day in Mumbai, and because of the time change, I'm trying to turn my days into my nights and my nights into my days. I don't take any sleeping aids. I give my body time to adjust, but I haven't had a solid night of sleep in the six months since my son died, and the result is constant jetlag. It's like not being fully grounded in time and space. It's a lot like grief.

I'm waking up here early in the morning, before 4:00 a.m. It's way before sunrise, so I make a cup of tea and open the curtains to reveal a full moon illuminating the Arabian Sea. Today is my sixtieth birthday.

I grab my laptop and start writing. I've done this every morning since Charlie died. I want to make peace with the unacceptable. I write through the sadness, and I write through the rage. Today is day 193.

I'm traveling alone, so the laptop is my company. The darkness of the early morning is my company. The ghost of my son is my company. Instead of being scared of my grief, writing is a way to listen, to try and understand why my son's life ended a few weeks after he turned twenty-seven.

Before Charlie died from a drug overdose, we'd talked about returning to India this year. I brought him to India nearly twenty years ago when he was eight. I was spending two weeks in Sikkim making a film, and he was not doing well in school (second grade), so his dad agreed that he could come with me. The film was never released, but that trip now seems like destiny. It was a trip we talked about taking again for the next twenty years. Now I am returning alone to offer some of his ashes to the Ganges River.

I've been divorced for twenty-three years. I've been single by choice for ten years. After the divorce, Charlie used to say to me, "It's you and me against the world, Momma." Even though I had three older children, it often felt like it was Charlie and me against the world. He lived between two houses and a growing family. He went from being the youngest of my four to being a middle child after his father had three more children with two more women. Since then, it's been hard for all of us to find the family we belong to. For almost twenty years, right up until his death, Charlie continued to tell me, "It's you and me, Momma." It was his way of letting me know he would always be there for me. We would always be there for each other—and then suddenly he died and was gone.

Lately I'm wondering where I belong, especially after Charlie's death. My other children are grown, and they are all in relationships and live across the country from me. It's wonderful to see their growth and to see them belonging to someone, not in the sense of being owned but of being seen and appreciated. They are wanted. They belong.

Last night in Mumbai, I went to a mindset meditation class. I'm alone during the days, writing, so every night I try to go to a social event to engage with others. A movie, a dance class, a sound healing—it doesn't matter, I just want to be around others after a solitary day. Let me make it clear, I'm not lonely here. Since Charlie died, I'm just more aware that I'm alone.

The mindset class was facilitated by a woman, Nahla, who used to be a singer in Bollywood until she lost her voice. I'm a storyteller, and for me that's the start of a good story. I used to be [fill in the blank], and now I'm [fill in the blank]. Losing her voice led Nahla to discover the power of using her mind to heal. And then, through her mindset, she found the power of her voice again. That's a great story. As a storyteller, I'm always looking for the twist that makes for a better ending. With Charlie's death, there is no better ending.

Just before class, I changed out of the hotel robe I'd been wearing all day and put on a dress. I brushed my hair for the first time that day and put on red lipstick, trying to look like more than a mother in grief. I walked down two flights of stairs and into the room with a sign that said, "Unstoppable with Nahla."

The class theme was Be Unstoppable. It was exactly what Charlie was at the end. I knew something was wrong. I hadn't heard from him in several days. I was hysterical as I called around to people who might know where he was, but they dismissed me and ignored my concerns. I always knew when someone was wrong with Charlie, but this time, he made it so I couldn't find him. He was unstoppable.

Everyone in the class was half my age, about the age of my children, about the age of Charlie when he died. I almost turned around to walk back upstairs, but Nahla greeted me and pointed to a yoga mat and pillow where I could sit in a circle with the group of thirty.

Nahla started by inviting us to share an intention with the group. The intention would become our mantra for the evening. When my turn came, I offered, "Belonging." I don't know why I chose that word for a mantra, it's what came up first. There I was in India, 8,000 miles from home, trying to remember how to belong to something other than sadness.

Nahla encouraged us to lie down and begin a meditation. I was so exhausted, the back of my body sank into my mat like the ground was swallowing me. As she spoke, I closed my eyes and opened them into the darkness of a deep space. Charlie appeared. A few days after he died, he came to me once in my dreams but nothing since. How did he find me in India?

Charlie was quiet as he reached for me and held me for a long hug, just like the last one we had before he died. I could feel the curve of his shoulders; I could feel the rise and fall of his breath. I could see him. Finally, Charlie was here again in my arms. It felt like belonging. When I hugged harder, his body disintegrated and poof, he was gone. I started to get upset until I noticed I was still supported by the energy of his arms around me and by the rise and fall of his breath. I felt the essence of the curve of his shoulders and my hands on his back. This time, I couldn't see him, but I still felt his presence right there in Mumbai under a full moon on the eve of my birthday. "Happy birthday, Momma," he whispered as I held onto nothing and everything. "I'm always with you. It's still you and me against the world."

Everyone came out of that meditation with their superpowered mantra. I came out of it with another moment with Charlie, another moment of belonging. Even in death, he was unstoppable. Maybe in his death, I can remember to be unstoppable too.

ANGELS IN
NEW MEXICO

I've never believed in angels, but my son Charlie did, especially the last few years of his life. Maybe it was being raised in a mostly white Christian church and going to a mostly black high school in Indianapolis, but I always questioned the narrative and images of lily-white angels. It seemed like some information and representation were missing. I believed in God/Goddess and the Divine, but I used to quietly roll my eyes when people talked about angels. Charlie was a believer though; his favorites were Raphael and Gabriel. He spoke of them like they were old friends.

In 2017, I met Madeline Giles, who was leading an Angelic Breath Meditation during a Qoya teachers' training in Taos, New Mexico. The intention was to connect to breath as a means to call in support from our angels. Before the meditation, others in the group had angel stories that I listened to but didn't really believe. I had low expectations for both the angels and the meditation.

We each lay down on a yoga mat and got comfortable, and then Madeline began the mediation. As her voice became a portal into a deep, relaxing space, I yawned, softened my shoulders, and treated it as potential nap time. I dropped deeper and deeper into a void as Madeline's voice guided us until her words disappeared, and I was suspended in a dark open space. Suddenly, I saw something dancing around me. Angels? Fairies? My imagination? They were giggling at me. They were making fun of me making fun of them. I watched the angels for a while, smiling at their playfulness, and then Madeline's voice came back into my space, and she asked the angels to reveal something to me that I needed to know. They quickly got serious and showed me a scene that made me want to turn away and escape them. The angels showed me that my son Charlie was alone and in pain. He brought a pill to his mouth, and then I witnessed his death, his body both dropping and lifting at the same time. The moment he transitioned, he was immediately surrounded by the angels who held onto him as they floated upward together into a soft white light.

When the meditation was over, Madeline asked us to thank the angels for whatever message we received. I didn't thank the angels; I was pissed at them for showing me my youngest son's death. And I was swallowing back tears because at the time, Charlie was twenty-two years old and a new dad. He was very much alive.

After the meditation, Madeline asked us to share anything that came up for us. I shared my experience with one person—and now I'm sharing it with you. I never told Charlie, although he would have loved it because he constantly talked to his angels.

Five years later, when Charlie's body was found alone in a hotel room, dead from a drug overdose, the memory of the meditation with Madeline brought me so much peace. He wasn't alone in death. He was surrounded by his angels.

GRACE

BALTO

It took four months for me to drive thirty minutes. It was to see Balto, my son Charlie's dog, who went to a new home after Charlie died. I wanted to keep Balto, but I lived in a Northern California rental property with no pets allowed. After Charlie died, I thought briefly about buying a home so I could keep his dog with me, but I knew a big change like a move wouldn't be advisable or even possible; I was barely moving through the days and weeks, sadness and grief holding me hostage.

Charlie was alone for at least two days before someone found him dead in a Sacramento hotel room. There are so many unacceptable things about his death, and knowing he was alone is one of them. And then I remembered Charlie wasn't alone—his Australian sheepdog, Balto, was with him. Australian sheepdogs are barkers, they are vocal. It was the one time we needed Balto to bark, and he didn't. It was also the one time we needed Charlie to ask for help and he didn't.

Charlie had been staying at the hotel for several weeks to be close to doctor's appointments. Anytime he left Balto alone in the hotel room, the front desk clerk called to tell him that the dog was barking and disturbing the nearby guests. Charlie always returned right away. Balto didn't like to be alone. Charlie didn't like to be alone. They were a good match.

Balto was a sweet dog who adored Charlie. He was only eighteen months old and had a beautiful coat of thick, wavy black fur. Charlie lived on a rural farm in Northern California where Balto had space to run, but in their short time together, he also joined Charlie on road trips. One was to Las Vegas, where they stayed at a posh hotel and ate room service. When they were together, Balto never barked. He was calm and chill, kind of like Charlie most days. Australian sheepdogs are loyal, especially to family. He slept with Charlie at night. When Charlie lay dead, Balto was next to his body, waiting for him to wake up. Charlie's body went to the coroner's office, and animal control officers took Balto to a shelter.

Because Charlie's death was under investigation, the coroner wouldn't let me see him until after the autopsy. They told me it would be a week or so. That was another unacceptable thing, that I couldn't see my son's body right away. I'd brought him into the world. I felt his heartbeat first inside my womb, and once he was born, I watched him take his first breath. I needed to be with him in death too. Harley also wanted to see him. She'd just turned twenty-four and now would be raising their two children, Sunny and Ray, on her own.

After we found out Charlie was dead, Harley and I spent the first forty-eight hours in a daze, allowing the girls to play between our two homes. Harley hadn't told the children yet, but they saw us crying, and they could sense the energy was different. I'd always told the girls that it was okay to cry, and it was okay to be sad, so they didn't let our tears scare them. Instead, they stayed close and drew pictures of fairies and rainbows and hearts, and they passed the pictures to us as offerings.

The first two nights I stayed at my house alone, crying myself to sleep and crying myself awake. Then, on Sunday afternoon, I got the urge to pick up Balto. I couldn't bring him to my house, so Harley agreed to take him. She had a big backyard where he could run. We decided I'd pick him up and bring him over and spend the night with her and the girls. I hadn't slept much, and I knew it would be easier to sleep cuddled next to Sunny and Ray. Maybe Balto would sleep with us too.

It was a hot Sunday afternoon when I stopped at Target for dog food and treats and toys and then drove to the animal shelter. I'd scribbled the address on the same piece of paper that held important notes and numbers I'd gathered since Charlie's death. I arrived at the shelter and gave Balto's case number. It was late in the day, and several couples were waiting to adopt pets. I watched as one of the adoptions was completed, and the staff brought the dog out. The pup wagged its tail and offered appreciative licks to its new owners. It brought me so much joy to watch, and I teared up knowing how sweet this reunion with Balto would be. I couldn't wait to see him, to hug him, and to take him on a walk. We'd heal together. Just then, the door opened to the waiting room; Balto saw me and lunged. I dropped to my knees, crying, to welcome his cuddles and kisses, but instead he was pulling at the leash and nipping at my arms, face, and anything that was within reach. It was the opposite of the adoption scene. Balto was crazed, like I'd done something to him. It was such a strong reaction that I'm surprised they sent him with me—it looked like he had retained a memory of something terrible I'd done to him, and he was ready to attack.

I'd already completed all the paperwork, so I quickly took him out the door, knowing he'd probably calm down with a walk. Outside, he continued to jump at me, wrapping his teeth around my arm, ready to bite if

I didn't pull away. I tried to walk with him, but he kept lunging at me, so I decided to get him into the car and try and calm him down with food and toys. He knew my car. He'd ridden in it a month earlier when I picked Charlie and him up. He knew me, but at that moment he seemed to be out of his mind.

I started to drive, remembering the last time he fell asleep in the back seat of my car while Charlie and I talked. Maybe the drive would soothe him. Instead, as I pulled onto the highway, Balto climbed from the back seat into the middle seat and then tried to jump into the front seat. I put up my arm to block him, to keep him in the middle seat. I was afraid if he got into the front, we'd crash. Just then, Harley called from her house, checking on my arrival time. We were all clinging to the idea that Balto would bring some comfort over the next few days. As she spoke, Balto was growling and pacing in the middle seat, like he was warming up for a fight. I finally said, "Can you call the animal shelter and tell them I'm bringing him back? He's very anxious and aggressive, and I don't think it's safe for him to be around the girls. I need to figure out another plan."

Harley hung up and then called back minutes later as I was exiting the highway to turn around to return to the shelter. "They just closed," she said, "and they won't take him back. Just bring him to the house and we'll keep him in the back yard until we can figure something out. He's just traumatized. He'll be okay."

I pulled to the side of the road and parked. I looked at Balto. His fur was falling out; there were chunks of his dark coat everywhere. His eyes looked a lot like mine— we both had brown eyes and the vacant stare that went with shock and sadness. "It's going to be okay, Balto," I whispered through tears. A wave of exhaustion hit us both at the same time. He settled down and I leaned my head back on the headrest and closed my eyes. After a few minutes, I started to drive again, keeping an eye on the dog in the rearview mirror. He was sound asleep.

When Harley and Charlie lived together, she was the one who did most of the dog care. Even though they'd lived apart for the past four years, since Ray was born, I admired them for continuing to show up for each other and for working to heal, even if they chose not to be together. Balto knew Harley and the girls. He'd be happy to see them.

Harley was waiting for us as I pulled into her driveway. "Go on inside with the girls," she said. "I'm going to give Balto a bath and then let him run in the backyard. He'll calm down. The girls are excited to see him. There's dinner for you in the kitchen."

She grabbed Balto's leash, and he sprang out of the car, pulling her towards his hysteria. I walked to the front door and into the house. The girls were freshly bathed, their long hair brushed into braids for the night. They were excited to have "Gogo" (my grandmother name) spend the night with them. They often spent the night at my house, but I had never stayed with them at theirs.

The girls ran to me with arms stretched up, and I picked them up together. Ray was four, Sunny was five. They were ten months apart, so almost like twins. Ray had dark hair and dark eyes like Harley, and Sunny had Charlie's light hair and blue eyes.

We went into their bedroom so I could change into my pajamas. My dress was covered in Balto's dark fur. I changed into a leopard-print pajama set, pants and a top. It was lightweight and perfect for hot summer nights. "Balto is here," I said to the girls. "Let's go see him."

I passed by the dinner waiting for me on the counter, and we headed for the sliding glass doors that went to the back yard. Harley had finished Balto's bath, and he was zooming around the backyard, non-stop. I'd never seen him behave like that. It was like he was on speed. We started to walk outside to greet him. He'd always been so good with the kids, but he jumped towards us, and I pushed the girls back inside. "Let's let him run it out,"

Harley said, and she came inside with us. As we shut the sliding door, separating us from Balto, he started barking aggressively and jumping on the glass. He was only sixty pounds, but he attacked the door and scratched at it with his front paws. We tried to close the curtain, but that made it even worse. He pounded at the door, throwing his body against it. "I'll sit outside with him until he calms down," I said. "Why don't you all start bedtime? I'll join you in a little bit."

I inched my way outside, talking Balto down from the high he was on. "Good boy, Balto. It's okay. I'm not going to leave you." He wrapped his teeth around my arm again but didn't bite down. I sat on a chair and put my other hand on his side, being careful not to make any quick moves. "It's okay. I'm here. You're okay, buddy. Good boy." After a few minutes, he finally let go and dashed back and forth across the yard again. He didn't want to play. He didn't want to catch a ball. He just wanted to run, probably from the trauma of the past few nights. I didn't have the energy to run. I was suddenly exhausted and finally felt I could sleep. I moved to a wicker loveseat on the patio, but the sudden move made Balto rush to me and grab my arm again with his teeth. "I'm right here. I'm not going anywhere," I said. "Good boy," I added as he loosened his grip.

I leaned back into the seat, tired and hungry because I hadn't eaten all day. I noticed Harley had turned off the lights in her bedroom, so at least the girls were able to have a normal bedtime routine. I'd sneak into the girls' room after I got Balto settled. He was lying down at my feet, and now he looked tired too. He was so loyal to Charlie, and these last days were so traumatic for him. I'm glad he could finally rest. I must have dozed off, too, because I woke up as the late summer sun was setting. I looked at my phone, and it was after nine p.m. I was hungry and needed to go to the bathroom. I slowly got up and stepped over the sleeping Balto to go inside. As I opened the door, he barked and jumped between me and the house. "I just need to go potty and eat some dinner, Balto, I'll be right back." I pushed my way around him and inside, but he jumped and barked as I slid the door shut. I didn't want him to wake the girls, so I quickly turned around and went out again. Dinner would have to wait. I walked to the side of the fenced garden, dropped my pajama bottoms, and peed.

The dog was now awake and in action again, running in circles around the yard. "It's okay, Balto, I'm here." He ignored me and ran faster, like he was in a trance. I inched my way slowly towards the door again, still wanting to go inside to eat, and he raced across the yard to stop me.

91

I returned to the wicker loveseat and grabbed a beach towel off a chair to use as a blanket. The temperatures cooled as the darkness set in. Balto watched me cover myself with the towel and then he lay down, right in front of the sliding door so I couldn't get past him, and he fell back asleep. I watched as his breathing slowed. Sometimes he whined like he was having a dream, sometimes his body twitched, sometimes he'd wake up to see if I was still there and then go back to sleep.

Other than my leopard pajamas, the only thing I had with me was my cell phone. I'd left my purse, shoes, and toiletries inside the house hours ago when I thought I'd be back inside in a few minutes. It was now eleven p.m., and I was cold. There were no other towels outside, so I sent Harley a text, asking her to bring out a blanket, hoping she'd wake in the middle of the night and read it. I couldn't risk going in for a few minutes and Balto going crazy and waking everyone up or damaging the door. He was in trauma just like the rest of us. Anytime I tried to get up, he jerked awake like my movements were an alarm for him. Every time he noticed that I didn't leave him, he would inch closer to me.

Balto hadn't let me pet him at all since I picked him up. I knew trauma didn't like to be touched; his nervous system was in fight-or-flight, and mine was in freeze mode. Finally, as the moon lit up the dark night, he moved towards me and put his head on my lap. I slowly placed my hand on his head and moved it lightly back and forth to pet him. He let out a big exhale, and then he crawled up into my lap. I don't know if dogs can cry, but at that moment, I knew I was crying, and it seemed like he was too.

"Thank you for being with Charlie," I said. "Thank you for staying by his side. Thank you for being a safe place for his pain. Thank you for being with him as he died. Thank you. Thank you. Thank you." I have been with three people as they died. All were in hospice care. It's an honor to be trusted as a safe place for someone to transition. Charlie did not die alone. He chose Balto.

That's when I decided to give up trying to go inside. Balto stayed by Charlie's dead body for two days. I'd stay by Balto for the night and let him know he was safe. His body on my lap provided some warmth as the ninety-degree day dropped into a fifty-degree night. "I'm right here," I said. "I'm not going anywhere. I'm not going to let your pain chase me away. It's okay now. You're safe. I love you. Good boy." I know at some point, the words I was whispering were meant for Charlie. "It's going to be okay. I'm here now. I love you. You're safe."

Balto and I were both jolted awake by a sound. The sprinkler system went off and was aimed right at the loveseat. Our nervous systems were both reactive, and I jumped up, cold and damp. My heart was racing. Balto started to run again. The towel was wet, my pajamas were wet. I looked at my phone. It was two a.m. There was no message from Harley. At least she and the girls were sleeping. I walked towards the door, this time thinking I could take Balto inside with me to look for a blanket or dry towel. He hustled over to stand in front of me and growled. His trauma was triggered again. I looked on the patio and found two mismatched seat cushions. I dried the wicker loveseat with the damp towel and then covered part of my body with the two cushions. I curled up into a ball and tried to sleep again with Balto at my feet. Sometime after four a.m., as the early sun was promising light, Harley came out with a blanket. "I just saw your message," she said. "I can't believe you were out here all night."

The long night and fatigue from the previous days made me feel like I was hungover. "I just need to go to the bathroom," I said. "Can you stay with him?" I stumbled inside. Balto let me go as long as Harley stayed. It felt like he was holding us hostage when really, he was just scared to be alone. I thought about some of Charlie's angry calls in the months before he died. It often seemed like he was holding us hostage with his attacks. Now I realized too late, he was just in trauma and scared to be alone.

It was warm in the house, and I wrapped a bathroom towel around me before I returned to the back yard. The girls were still asleep. Harley had moved into the house three months ago, and I knew she had her old couch in the garage. "He won't stay alone, and I need to sleep more. Can we put us in the garage so I can stay warm?" I said. "And then in a few hours, I'll try to find a kennel that can take him for a few days. If I take him back to the shelter, I'd have to surrender him, and I don't want to put him through any more trauma."

Harley helped me move into the garage with Balto and brought me a blanket and a warm cup of tea. He climbed onto the couch with me, and we both slept for a few hours. By 6:30 a.m., I was up again and in the car with him. I was completely drained. I didn't want the girls to be at risk with the dog's unsteady behavior, so I left the house before they were awake. I was still in my leopard-print pajamas. I watched the sun rise as I drove into another day of a road trip with grief. I drove ten minutes and parked at the top of a hill overlooking the Sierra Mountain range and rivers, where prospectors first discovered gold in the 1850s. I'd never spent any time in Northern California, and now it was the place of my greatest joy, my granddaughters, and my greatest sorrow, the death of my youngest son. I looked in the rearview mirror, and Balto was peacefully sitting on the seat staring at the sunrise too.

I know that dogs can take on the energy or illness of their owners. I've heard stories and I've seen it happen, from cancers that transferred from the owners to their animals to depression that lifted after the companionship of a new puppy. Whatever Balto and I went through that night was a journey through the darkness, and now we were both sitting with each other, watching for the light. We were both watching for Charlie.

"Charlie," I said. "Please show me what's best for Balto. If I'm meant to keep him, show me how. If he's meant to be with someone else, show me who."

Balto laid his head back on the seat and slept as I made a call to my three older children. Sam and Willie were in Indiana, and Lucy was on her way there, where we all planned to gather in ten days to celebrate the life of their little brother.

"I need your help finding a local kennel for Charlie's dog. I can't take him to my rental home, and I'm too exhausted to look for places. We're sitting in the car because we didn't sleep much last night, and we have nowhere to go. And I'm still in my pajamas."

I'm sure I sounded unsettled. I stared at the sleeping Balto, sending him love and any healing I had left in my own broken spirit. Within an hour, Sam sent suggestions for local kennels. None had space for a dog, especially one without papers. I had no idea if he had the required immunizations. I had no idea where Balto came from. Charlie was always taking on dogs that no one wanted.

"We found a place!" Lucy texted a few minutes later from Connecticut. She was with her partner, Tess, and her best friend, Kailee. Together they worked their magic and found a kennel that had day and night boarding. Normally they accepted only dogs who had been with them for day boarding, but in Balto's case, they would make an exception. The owner, Jennifer, a certified dog trainer, was willing to meet him first, and if he did okay, he could stay as a boarder for a few days. I texted her and she said to come in an hour.

An hour later we arrived at the kennel. As I stepped out of my car, I looked down at my leopard-print pajamas and black sandals. My contacts from the day before were dry against my blood-shot eyes. Jennifer met me at the car. She didn't know about last night, she only knew the dog had some trauma around the death of his owner. Balto got out of the car and immediately jumped on her, but it was a playful jump, nothing like the attacks I'd experienced.

"I'm going to take him around one of our greeter dogs to see how he does, and then we'll decide if he can stay."

Balto walked next to her, wagging his tail. He sniffed the greeter dog, Rosie. Rosie sniffed back. "He's doing great," Jennifer said. "No aggression. He's doing well." She watched him interact with Rosie for a few minutes and said, "I'll keep him for the day. If he does okay, he can stay a few nights."

"Thank you," I said, almost weepy to leave him. I was completely worn out and needed to sleep and eat, so I left his food and toys and drove away.

Balto ended up staying there almost a month. I had to be in Indiana twice that month, first for the services for Charlie and then to return with some of his ashes for his father, who lived in Indiana. Jennifer often sent me text updates to let me know how Balto was doing. "He's doing great. He's a sweet dog." I shared the updates with my kids and Harley. During such a big loss, Balto's ability to thrive beyond the trauma was such a big win.

Charlie had Balto for the last eighteen months of his life, and in many ways, Balto probably extended his life by keeping him company and making him feel secure in a world that didn't always feel safe. Charlie named Balto after a real dog who became a hero in 1925 as the lead sled dog to deliver serum to a remote, snowed-in community in Alaska. His efforts saved many children who were sick with diphtheria. Balto was a lifesaver.

In the same magical way, we found a home for Balto on a farm twenty-two miles from where I lived. It was a house on twenty acres with an extraordinary patient and kind retired couple, John and Julie. They had just moved into their dream home and were looking for a dog to adopt. They wanted to give a dog a forever home. Balto deserved that forever home.

The day before Julie and John picked him up from the kennel, I went to see Balto and say goodbye. He ran to greet me but also stayed close to Jennifer. I appreciated that she'd been a safe place for him to heal. He was with Charlie when he died, and it wouldn't have been fair to Balto to move in with me and take on my pain and grief. He deserved joy, and that is exactly what he got in his new home.

John and Julie gave me an open invitation to visit anytime, and I finally went the week before Thanksgiving. After Charlie's death, it was hard to find gratitude, but I wanted to extend my gratitude to this couple who took a chance on Balto.

It had been four months since he and I spent that long, dark night together. When I arrived to visit, as I got out of my car, Balto stood up and cocked his head. His fur was thick and shiny. He looked so healthy! As I walked to him, he playfully jumped and nipped at me. I was so concerned that he wasn't being a "good dog" for them, but right away, Julie started talking to him and telling Balto all the great things about him. She told him she loved him so much, and this was his forever home. She reminded him that even in the moments he jumped or didn't follow the rules, he was still worthy of love and attention. Balto calmed right down and finally brought me his toy. He put it on my leg, wanting to play.

They take Balto on two hour long walks every day and never leave him alone. "That's what he needs," Julie said. "He doesn't like to be alone. He needs to run. He needs to be reminded he has a forever home." She was telling me about Balto, but she could have been talking about Charlie and anyone who is struggling. They don't need to be yelled at or sent away. They need to be reminded they are still wanted, even on their bad days. Charlie knew this because from a young age, he was always bringing home puppies and dogs who needed extra attention. He always saw the good in pets—and in people—whom others saw as damaged or wounded or not worth getting close to. Even when others didn't want them, Charlie let them know that they still mattered. He was a lifesaver for others. And Balto was a lifesaver for Charlie.

SMOKE SIGNALS

My youngest son Charlie was bad at hiding things. He always got caught. The summer he turned sixteen, he secretly started to smoke. His bedroom in our home in Indiana was directly above mine, so I always knew when he was smoking. Charlie usually smoked at night when he thought I was asleep, but the odor would wake me, and I'd go upstairs to try and open his locked door. I could hear him closing the window, and then I'd smell the cologne he was spraying in the room to cover the smoke. I knew exactly what he was doing.

"Charlie, I know you've been smoking. I can smell it."

He would open the door with a smile on his face. "Mom, smoking tobacco is sacred. It's a way to pray."

Charlie always had an answer that could potentially make sense. It's true, in indigenous cultures for thousands of years, smoking was considered sacred. But we lived in a modest Nantucket-style lake home close to shopping malls and popular restaurants in Indianapolis. We didn't go to church. I'm pretty sure he wasn't praying between puffs on his American Spirit cigarettes.

Charlie was the youngest of my four children. I separated from their father when he was two and was divorced by the time he was four. It was not enough time for him to feel rooted in the family. Maybe he was looking for other ways to connect to someone or something.

"So, what were you praying about?" I asked when he finally opened his door.

"That you wouldn't catch me smoking."

It was hard to be upset with Charlie for very long because he always had a big comeback or big story or big plan or big smile that he used to redirect your attention. He was always searching for meaning—and he was always searching for a good time.

"Next time, you can dance," I said. "That's a form of prayer too." And so, Charlie reached for me and did a little dance, and then we said good night. The next morning, he asked if he could have a party at the house for his sixteenth birthday.

"Just forty people or so," he asked. "I promise, no smoking or drinking. We just want to hang out and listen to music."

His birthday was soon, on July 17. His siblings were going to be away. His oldest brother, Sam, was studying in Italy for the summer, and Lucy and Willie were working as camp counselors. That's what often happens when you are the youngest—family celebrations and traditions get smaller as the older siblings leave home. I didn't want Charlie to be alone on his birthday, so of course I said yes.

"But only twenty friends," I said. "Forty is too many for the house."

"Okay thirty it is," Charlie replied. "Thanks, Momma."

"I said twenty!"

"Twenty is not even a party. How about twenty-five? And I'll clean up."

Two weeks later, as the first of twenty-five guests arrived, I was preparing snacks for the party. I put out an ice-filled tub on the patio with water and sodas, plus buffalo chicken dip and mini-BBQ sandwiches, all Charlie's favorites. His birthday cakes were always the same—chocolate cake with rich, dark chocolate frosting.

"Thanks, Momma, for the food and drinks," he said. "My buddies and I are going to be down at the dock."

Our home overlooked a small lake. There was a large patio off the kitchen with great lake views and steps down to a dock. The dock held only five or six people, so most of the party would be on the upper patio where I could keep an eye on the action. More friends arrived through the front door, and each one greeted me.

"Hi, Mama B… Hi, Betsy!" Some were new friends, but I had known many for at least five years. They were all good kids.

I kept busy putting more food and drinks out. I was the only adult at the party. Charlie's dad was busy with another child who was five years old and yet another one on the way. Both with different mothers. Charlie had gone from being the youngest in our family to being in between. He was in between children and families and homes. It was confusing to all of us. He'd had a hard few years trying to process the changes. I wanted this night to be special for him.

Just after the sun set at 8:30 p.m., I lit sixteen candles on Charlie's cake, and we all sang to him. He was so happy. By now, there were at least forty people at the party. Charlie always seemed to get his way, but it was okay. He was also very appreciative and kept checking in.

"Thanks for everything, Momma," he said with both words and hugs. "Thanks for my party."

Charlie had blue eyes that sparkled like his father's. This was the first year he was taller than me. He wore a favorite blue and white Hawaiian shirt open to the navel. He'd started getting chest hair recently and was proud to show it off.

Every so often, I'd make the rounds outside and was so impressed that everyone was following the no-drinking and smoking rules. They were happy drinking water. Some even brought their own water bottles. Even though I'd raised three other teenagers, it never occurred to me that there was anything other than water in the bottles.

As the sky got darker, I reminded Charlie and his friends to keep the music low, otherwise the neighbors would complain. "No problem, Mama Betsy," said his friend Sam as he promptly turned the music down from the switch inside the kitchen. The party was to end at 11:00 p.m. At 10, I made a cup of tea to keep awake. I was so impressed that the party was going so well. Just one more hour.

As the waning full moon lit the skies, I noticed that the patio looked crowded, but no one else had come in through the front door. I felt the heightened energy before I saw them, and then suddenly there was a line of people flowing in from the right side of the house. And they looked much older than Charlie's friends.

I heard laughter and loud voices from the other direction. I ran to the other side of the house and saw even more people. They were appearing from both sides like an ambush. There were well over a hundred people on my small deck and a cloud of tobacco and marijuana rising out of the crowd. Just then the doorbell rang. I could see blue flashing lights through the front windows. I looked through the back window at Charlie, who was right in the middle of everyone, smiling and dancing like it was the best night of his life.

I shut the music off and shouted, "Charlie!"

He came in looking like he couldn't talk his way out of what he was about to tell me.

"Mom, a little problem. Someone put the address of the party on Twitter."

"Was that someone you?"

The doorbell rang again. We walked together to open the front door.

"Momma, don't be mad, it's my sixteenth birthday."

Charlie was smart enough not to drink that night, so when he met the police at the front door with me, he explained the situation. Like I said, Charlie could talk his way out of anything. He invited the police in for cake.

The officers asked everyone who had someone sober driving to leave. They walked around the outside of the house and found bottles of vodka and gin in the bushes. I realized the kids weren't just drinking water; they had been refilling their bottles from the shrubbery. Inside the house, the officers saw the cake and snacks and cup of tea—and no alcohol. It was clear to them that I wasn't knowingly hosting an underage drinking party.

After the police left, Charlie and I turned the music back on low and cleaned up the patio. I watched him find an opened pack of Camel cigarettes, and instead of throwing them in the trash, he tucked them in the pocket of his shirt.

"Charlie," I said as I extended my hand to him for the cigarettes.

"Mom, I told you, cigarettes are for prayers, it's like sending a smoke signal."

"Smoking is bad for your lungs," I said. "Please pray with something else."

He smiled and handed over the pack. I tossed them into the trash. It was past midnight, and I was tired.

"That was the best party ever," Charlie said. "Let's dance, Momma."

And so, we danced to imperfect birthdays and imperfect families, under a full moon that still managed to shine in so much darkness.

Just after his next birthday when he turned seventeen, Charlie moved to California, and for the next several years, we were rarely together on his birthday. Often, we celebrated months later, but we always celebrated. During that time, Charlie was excelling in work as a cannabis farmer and consultant, and he was also trying to move on from the wounds of the past and accept family dynamics that looked very different from the one he was born into.

On his twenty-first birthday, he was thrilled to tell me he was going to be a father. He'd fallen in love with Harley, a California girl with a golden heart. By his twenty-second birthday, they had a four-month-old daughter named Sunny and another on the way. I hoped that in raising young children, he could heal the wounds from his own childhood. He was estranged from some of his birth family but always wanting to heal. Instead, he started showing up less and less for Harley, and he got better at hiding things—his increased drug and alcohol use, his depression, his discouragement, his distrust. And he was hiding the shame of unexpressed trauma. He was hiding, but I always felt him, and I always found him and then reminded him that it was going to get better after he got through the pain. Once, he called in despair, so I asked him what he needed. "Can you just come and give me a hug?" I got into my car and drove forty-five minutes to see him. By the time I arrived, he was passed out.

A few months after that, Charlie turned twenty-five. I showed up at his house to celebrate his birthday with a cake and candles in the shape of the numbers twenty-five. "Mom, I'm turning twenty-four," he said. I quickly ran the numbers in my head. "You were born in 1995," I said. "It's 2020, so you are twenty-five today." We laughed about the birthday mix-up, but the drive home from seeing him brought tears. How do you lose a year of your life? Charlie had a brilliant mind, but he often disappeared into the poison of the pain and into a brain that was increasingly unbalanced. Sometimes he scared us; often he scared himself. Twice that year he nearly lost his life from taking unprescribed Xanax. Twice he promised me he'd never take Xanax again.

The next summer, when Charlie turned twenty-six, his birthday gifts sat on my table until October. He was working hard to survive physically, emotionally, spiritually, and financially. He'd lost some big deals with work, and he was losing more pieces of himself through drugs. When we finally did celebrate, Charlie came to dinner at my house with Harley and their girls, Sunny and Ray. He and Harley were no longer living together, but they continued to show up for each other when they could, even as pieces of their love story were disappearing with Charlie into the darkness. One year later, ten days after his twenty-seventh birthday, Charlie was found dead of a drug overdose.

I often caught Charlie getting into trouble when he was younger, but in the last days of his life, he made sure I couldn't catch him. I knew something was wrong. I was searching for him for days, but he was already gone.

The morning after Charlie was found dead in a hotel room, I woke up to the smell of someone smoking in my home. I lived alone. The last time that happened was eleven years earlier when Charlie lived with me. He knew he wasn't allowed to smoke in the house—or even to smoke—so when I smelled it the morning after he died, I knew it was him. "Where are you, Charlie...where are you?" I whispered. I'd cried myself to sleep the night before, and then I cried myself awake. I still couldn't believe he was gone.

It made me remember being in Zimbabwe and learning from a shaman, a local woman who was a medicine doctor, that smoking can be a ritual, like a prayer, just like Charlie had once told me. I did not smoke, but the shaman gave me a pack of cigarettes and said to use them as a form of prayer. Over the course of several weeks, I slowly smoked each cigarette, praying as I inhaled and releasing the prayers as I exhaled. By the time I finished the pack, I understood how our culture had taken an ancient ritual and turned it into a bad habit. Each inhale was an intention, and every exhale was sending my prayers out into the world. After that, I never took up smoking, but when I needed to, I used tobacco as a sacred medicine as our ancestors had intended it.

When I smelled the smoke the morning after Charlie was found dead, I knew he was sending out his prayers and was finally at peace. And he was sending a smoke signal to let me know he was okay and to remind me if I wanted to stay close to him, I just needed to dance.

GOOD-LUCK CHARLIE

It's been four years since the divorce, and the other kids are adjusting, but my youngest, Charlie, wants us all together. He wants his family. I understand—I want to feel like a family again too. I'm against the arrangement of the two older boys living at their dad's and Lucy and Charlie living with me, but that becomes the plan as they begin the new school year. Often it feels like I've lost both my family and my voice.

Charlie is starting second grade. Right away he is having challenges. His teacher invites us to a conference, and her recommendation is shocking. She urges us to put him on Adderall, a pharmaceutical, to help him focus. She tells us she takes it herself. Adderall is a Class II narcotic, the same category as cocaine and morphine and fentanyl. Charlie is eight.

Adderall will help him, his teacher pleads. He won't sit still; he won't pay attention. His dad is all for it, but I fight against it. His teacher is only telling us how to "fix" him; she never asks what happened to him or any reasons why he might not be able to focus. And since when should teachers be suggesting and encouraging medication?

Charlie was the easiest infant and child until age three. That's when we lost a baby I delivered at twenty weeks, and then lost our marriage within the same year. We lost our family. I lost myself. Charlie lost his foundation and connection to everything that made him feel stable and safe and like he belonged. So now, I hear a lot about what is wrong with Charlie from teachers and caregivers and family. I don't hear enough about what is right with him. I don't hear enough about how the wounds of the family could be impacting him. When a plant is dying, we check the soil, we check the water, we check the roots. We change the container, and we put the plant in more light. His teacher is telling us to medicate him when what he needs is to feel connected at the roots, to the family. He needs more light, more love. He needs our light, our love.

In the coming months, I try everything. Doing yoga at home with him before school. Starting him in a new karate class with Keith, an instructor who always sees the best in him. Being mindful of his diet. No soft drinks. I try to reduce dairy and sneak fish oil into his pancakes to strengthen his brain and focus. He is too smart and figures it out: "Stop putting healthy stuff into my pancakes, Mom!"

When Charlie spends nights at his dad's so he can be with his brothers, he misses Lucy and me and has trouble sleeping. His dad puts a large TV in his room, and he sleeps with it on all night. By second semester, his grades and spirit and energy are low. I'm thinking of canceling an upcoming two-week trip to India for work because I don't want to leave him.

It's easy to get Lucy ready for school. She's twelve and in seventh grade. She's already dressed and having breakfast while I'm still trying to get Charlie out of bed. This morning I woke up with the urge to take him to India with me. Butch, his dad, will never go for it. I release the idea and make a bath for Charlie. Like me, he loves morning baths. He stumbles down the stairs to the bath in my bedroom. I light a lavender candle, lower the lights, and leave his pancakes on the edge of the tub. I hope the gentle start to the morning will reduce the stress of the school day. Ten minutes later, Charlie's out of the bath, smiling, dressed, and ready to go. The kids get into our white VW SUV, and we head to school. It's a short drive and as we get closer, I see the smile drop from Charlie's face. He gets out of the car and shuffles towards the building with hunched shoulders. I wish I could make it better for him. How can I make it better for him?

I decide to ask Butch to let me take him to India, and I'm stunned when he agrees. Seriously. Stunned. He rarely agrees with me on anything. Sometimes I wonder how we both said yes to the vows at our wedding. He usually makes the opposite choice of whatever I want to do. When Charlie gets home from school, I ask him if he wants to join me on the trip. His big smile says yes before he does and so I buy Charlie a ticket to go with me to India. It doesn't solve the problems at school, but I hope it takes some pressure off him, because for the past six months, he's been taken to counselors and psychologists and doctors. All of them want to medicate him. No one is going to give my kid a drug. No one is going to medicate his magic.

India is an ambitious trip for anyone, especially an eight-year-old. Charlie is a chicken-finger and ketchup-loving child who will suddenly be living on rice and vegetables for two weeks. He says he'll be fine as long as I bring soy sauce for the rice. As we prepare to leave for India, I can sense him getting his good vibes back. I'm going to miss my other kids, but it's going to be great to share India with my youngest son.

We have two long flights ahead of us. The trip to get from Indiana to India will take us almost twenty-four hours. My only rule for him on the plane is that he can have one Coke during each flight. My only rule for him during the trip is that he will read two books and write in a trip journal every day, which will count towards his schoolwork.

Ten days later, we are off. Charlie is a great travel partner. He is immediately popular with the Virgin Airlines flight attendants. It helps that he's an adorable child with shaggy light brown hair, freckles, and a smile filling up with new teeth. We are sitting in their Upper Class cabin which is like business class. The seats are bigger, and there is even a small bar in our cabin, a place to sit and have a drink and snacks during the flight. Up until now, I've only traveled with his siblings throughout the U.S. on two- and three-hour flights in small economy class seats. Before we even take off, Charlie sinks into his seat by the window, buckles his seatbelt, plugs in the headphones, turns on a movie, and presses the flight attendant button. Before I can turn it off and ask him what he needs, someone appears. "May I have a Coke, please?" he says. "In a big glass." For the first time in a long time, Charlie looks happy.

On the first flight, from Chicago to London, I fall asleep. Charlie doesn't need to use the call button again because the flight attendants are always checking on him. I wake up every so often and see him watching a movie with his glass of Coke nearly full. I finally catch them refilling the Coke and remind him of the one-Coke rule. "You said one glass," he says. "It's the same glass!" Charlie is clever like that, following the rules and also finding ways to break them.

On our second flight from London to Delhi we have dinner and then both Charlie and I recline our seats and watch a movie on our personal screens. He's been so good to travel with so far. I peek over at him and he yawns so I close my eyes and go to sleep knowing he'll doze off soon too. When I wake up a few hours later, Charlie is not in his seat. The cabin is dark and quiet. It's the middle of the night, and everyone else is asleep. I look at the restroom lights and they are green, which means unoccupied. I get up and walk towards the galley, and there is Charlie, sitting at the bar and chatting with the flight attendants, his legs dangling off the high barstool. He has a dish of chocolate ice cream in front of him. He introduces me to the flight attendants like he's a seasoned traveler.

Three hours later, we land in Delhi and take one more flight, less than two hours, to Bagdogra airport in West Bengal. On that flight, Charlie doesn't have a Coke, he sleeps. I put my scarf around him, pull him close, and I match my breath with his, inhale and exhale, inhale and exhale. I always used to do that when he was a baby sleeping next to me or when he started to cry. I'd be intentional about matching his breath until he calmed down.

In Bagdogra, we are joined by Coulter, the videographer for the project I'm working on. At the airport,

I randomly hire a car to drive us four and a half hours to Sikkim. It's close to the border with Tibet, or what used to be Tibet until the Chinese Cultural Revolution in the 1950s. I've been to Sikkim once before, just last year, to produce and direct a documentary film with a lama who escaped Tibet in the 1950s. This trip, we are completing the filming. We're not here as tourists. It's an ambitious schedule, and as I review the details with Coulter, I wonder if it was a mistake to bring Charlie.

The drive takes us higher and higher into the mountains on narrow, rocky roads with no guard rails. If we need to pass another car, one of the vehicles hugs the mountain so the other can pass by. Several times we pass big passenger buses, and it doesn't seem possible for both of us to share the road. I close my eyes as we inch around each other, the wheels of our car dangerously close to the edge and a sheer drop. Charlie sleeps the whole way.

We arrive at the monastery just in time for lunch. Charlie looks at the plain white rice and greens in front of him and asks for the soy sauce. I look in my backpack and realize I forgot it. I'd packed a gallon bag full of individual soy sauces for the trip, and I accidentally left it at home. I brought other snacks, but I forgot the soy sauce for his rice, our main meal each day. At first, I can tell that he wants to cry, but he looks at the young monks his

117

age eating their plates of food without complaining, and he does the same.

The first week is spent filming at the monastery. It's framed by the Himalayan mountains with prayer flags flying in all directions. Charlie and I share a single wooden cot, smaller than a twin mattress, and sleep in our jackets and socks because it's so cold. The bathroom is a shared outhouse. I'm uncomfortable—I'd love to be in a luxury hotel, but none of this bothers Charlie. In the mornings, while I'm still sleeping, he climbs out of bed and finds the smaller kitchen, a wood shack, where the monks his age are making tea. The children cook for themselves. Charlie loves that they get to make a fire, especially because I'm always telling him not to play with matches. He doesn't speak Hindi and the young monks don't speak English, so they find the shared language of children.

At home, it's hard to wake Charlie up to go to school, but during the week at the monastery, he's up before me every day helping the young monks chop wood. His teacher complains that Charlie won't sit still in class, but in India he sits still for three to four hours in the temple when we are filming. It's been several years since I've seen him so content—both playful and at peace.

On the final day of production, we drive several hours to film at a cave that is known to be a place of enlighten-

ment for Tibetan monks. We leave after an early breakfast, and the plan is to be back at the monastery for
lunch. The filming takes longer, and I don't pack enough
snacks for Charlie. And then it starts to rain. And then
our camera batteries die. We're all cold and damp as we
load up the unheated car to drive the two hours back to
the monastery. The roads are uneven and wind around
the mountain. There are no seatbelts. We jokingly call
Charlie's dad Mr. Safety because of his commitment
to preventing dangerous situations. Butch wouldn't be
happy with either the car or the road conditions. The dirt
roads are packed with broken rock for traction, and often
the tires send stones flying off the edge of the cliffs. I look
away from the side of the road because it's too scary to
imagine going off into the void just a few feet from the
worn tires of the jeep.

Charlie starts to cry. He is tired and hungry and wet
and cold. I have nothing to offer him except my own wet
and cold arms around him. I try to coregulate with my
breath but he cries harder. Up until this moment, he's
been so good on this trip—there haven't been any tears,
but now they won't stop. "I'm so hungry," he keeps crying.
Due to the rain, we are having to drive slowly along the
treacherous roads. There are no places to stop for food
and gas; we pass tiny houses and shacks every so often.
After thirty minutes of his tears, our driver, who speaks

little English, pulls over and stops in front of a lopsided wooden home hanging on the edge of the mountain. He leaves us in the car and disappears inside the house. Now I am getting irritated. Can't he understand that we need to get back to the monastery? I hug Charlie closer to try and keep him warm.

A few minutes later, the driver returns and waves for us to come into the home. Now I'm really aggravated; I just want to get back to the monastery to change and eat. I try to tell him that, but he doesn't understand enough English, so we walk inside the home. It's one room with exposed windows that open to the mountains. The vision of the snow capped Himalayas is stunning. A couple motions for us to sit down at the table. It's one of the few pieces of furniture in the house. The table is a long piece of wood covered with a clean but faded blue tablecloth. We sit on a low bench, and the woman hands me a wool blanket. She has warmed it next to a fire. I wrap it around Charlie, and he sinks into it.

Three cups of hot water are set on the table for us. A young girl about Charlie's age hands us an orange. I can't ask the driver what is happening because we don't speak a common language. I assume the family are friends of his, and they invited us into their home to warm up. It feels lucky that we found them. I peel the orange, and Charlie, Coulter, and I share the pieces. I look out the window and see the rain has stopped, and the sun is beginning to peek through the clouds.

None of us speak a common language so we just smile and nod. I look around the home. There is the kitchen table and a small cot for sleeping but no other furnishings. The couple is cooking, and within minutes, huge plates of fried rice appear in front of us. Charlie's eyes get big. We've been eating plain white rice for a week at the monastery. He loves fried rice. He digs right in.

We all eat until our stomachs are full and our clothes are dry with the framed mountains watching us. The family doesn't eat; they watch us too. Our bodies are warmed from the inside and out. As the driver waves for us to leave, I offer money to the couple for the food. They won't accept it. They must be good friends of the driver, I think. Charlie's smile is back. He stands and reverently puts his hands together, brings them to his heart, and bows to the family like he's observed the monks doing this past week. He's never done it before. We giggle at his formality but he is not trying to be funny. It seems like Charlie has connected to something bigger. The family smiles and bows back, and then we leave.

It's another hour to the monastery and we drive in silence. Charlie falls asleep in my arms, warm and full of fried rice and love. Later, through a translator, I tell the driver to please thank his friends who fed us. He responds that he'd never met them. He just told them that my son was hungry, and that was enough for them to welcome us into their home and feed us. I wonder how school could be different for Charlie, if his teacher—and the therapists and counselors and doctors—looked for ways to welcome him into what he needs to feel supported instead of trying to medicate him.

Even though he doesn't speak Hindi, Charlie has made many new friends during the week of filming. The next day as we prepare to leave the monastery, the elder lamas and young monks line up to wave goodbye. As our car begins to pull away, Charlie tosses his favorite soft nerf football from the car to the monks. A young monk catches it and they all cheer. The elder and more reserved lamas smile. No one there tells me what is wrong with Charlie. Everyone sees his light.

Before we fly back to the US, I decide to take Charlie to visit a Bengal tiger preserve. We'll be staying in tents, but luxurious tents with bathrooms and a king-size bed. So far, the trip has focused on my work. I want to give Charlie an opportunity to see a side of India that will be of interest to him. He loves tigers.

It's five hours back to the airport, a three-hour flight, and then another two hours in a car to the tiger preserve. We check in and learn that no tigers have been seen for two weeks. I'm so disappointed. Charlie is disappointed until he learns the chef will make pizza for him. He is delighted to be back on a western diet.

From the outside, our room looks like a large tent, but when you enter, it's filled with all the comfort you find in a beautiful hotel. There's a living room, a bedroom, and a huge bathroom with a sunken tub.

After dinner, a beautiful hot bath is ready when we return to the tent. It's filled with soft bubbles and lit with candlelight. I know they prepared it for me, but Charlie gets in first, so I let him take a long bath, one of his favorite things. When he's done, he walks out of the bathroom with one of the adult ropes wrapped around his tiny body. He shuffles into the bedroom in the bath slippers, smiling and smelling like lavender. By the time I finish my bath, he is cozy in bed and sound asleep.

The next morning, we get up for the early morning drive into the tiger preserve. The game drives are in open-air jeeps. The most important rule is to sit still and stay quiet. This is potentially not an easy task for a kid whose teachers have told him that he is too active.

We knew they hadn't seen tigers in a few weeks, but that morning we see three tigers. Everyone is thrilled. We go again in the late afternoon and see six tigers. Now we are feeling lucky. I'm so glad Charlie got to see Bengal tigers in the wild. He requests pizza and a candlelit bath again tonight.

Tomorrow is our final day at the tented resort, so I decide we'll skip the game drives since we already saw the tigers. Charlie has made friends with the staff, especially the women in the kitchen who are spoiling him with pancakes and pizza and anything else he requests. This is more of an adult resort, so they are thrilled to have Charlie around, and he is loving the attention. The manager of the property invites Charlie to meet puppies that live onsite. I book a massage for the next day knowing the staff will entertain my son. After the massage, we'll check out and head to the airport to start the journey home.

At dinner, Charlie enjoys another cheese pizza, and I have curry. I'm loving this time with him but also missing my kids back home. Charlie is missing them too. At bedtime, we read a book, *The Kids' Joke Book,* because Charlie wants to be a comedian like his dad. Unlike when he's at home and believes he needs a TV, tonight he falls asleep easily. Since the divorce, he always seems a little stressed. It's good to see him content, especially because we are flying back to Indiana tomorrow. Maybe things will be better for him when we return.

When I wake up after sunrise, Charlie is not in the bed we are sharing. I get up and look around the tent. No Charlie. I throw on a robe and run outside to look for him, but he is not around. Now panicking, I run to the front desk for help.

"Oh, Mister Charlie went on the sunrise game drive."

I'm thinking, *You let him go by himself?* He's been gone for at least two hours. Just then the jeep pulls through the gate, and there is Charlie, sitting in the front seat, wearing his oversized white robe with binoculars hanging around his neck. Both he and the guide wave.

"Charlie is our good-luck charm," the driver says as he unloads two other guests who were in the jeep. "We saw ten Bengal tigers this morning. The most we've seen in a long time. Charlie is good luck."

Charlie smiles even bigger.

"And he was the best assistant guide. He sat very still and helped spot them. Now we call him Good-Luck Charlie."

Charlie hops out of the jeep and gives me a hug.

"Ready for breakfast?" I ask. "We leave for the airport after checkout in a few hours."

"No, I have breakfast plans," he says before trotting off to have breakfast with the kitchen staff.

After eating alone, I peek into the kitchen, and Charlie is seated at a high table, having his special breakfast. He's surrounded by staff, and he looks rooted in love, like he's discovered the pieces that are missing back home. In Indiana, he was constantly moving between two homes and two dinner tables. At school and in therapy, no one focused on what was right with him, only what was wrong with him. In India, no one sees Charlie as lacking anything, and he feels it. In India, they see him only as Charlie, as good luck, as good.

It's twenty years later and I've just arrived in India. A driver picks me up at the Mumbai airport to drive me to my hotel. It's late, almost midnight, and parts of the city come awake at night, so as we drive, I take photos out the window of nothing and everything.

"What are you photographing?" the driver asks.

"I'm taking photos for my son," I say. "He loves India."

I don't tell him more. I don't tell him that Charlie's ashes are next to me in my bag on the seat. Ten days after his twenty-seventh birthday, Charlie died of an overdose.

His pre-teen and teen years were spent between two homes and two families and too many schools that he was asked to leave. When he finally agreed to get a prescription for Adderall, he told me it was his legal drug. I was against it. Later, he was offered a prescription for Xanax. Charlie first found the drugs an escape from what he couldn't control; later they began to control him. Those drugs never fixed him like the teacher promised, they only did more damage.

My son dying alone in a California hotel room was not my dream for his life. When people ask me what he died from, saying that it was an overdose and fentanyl doesn't feel like the truth, because parts of Charlie started dying a long time ago of disappointment, disillusionment, and betrayal. If you've experienced physical, emotional, and mental trauma like Charlie did, it makes it harder to recover, so you reach for a drug or a bottle instead of telling the truth.

Just months before Charlie was found dead, he decided to detox from the drugs and alcohol, which in many ways had been a replacement for his family. During that time, he wrote to me a lot as he made peace with his past. We also spoke on the phone and in person. It was good to have my Charlie back.

We talked about returning to India together this year. We talked about going back to the monastery in Sikkim to see the young monks he'd met when he was a child. We talked about trying to find the home of the family that made fried rice for him when he was hungry. We talked about the tiger preserve and being called Good-Luck Charlie. We talked about how kind the people in India were to him. "I'm glad I didn't have a normal childhood," he said. But I wonder, if he'd had a normal childhood, would he still be alive?

After Charlie died, I decided to still make the trip with him and bring his ashes to the Ganges River, a place where Hindus believe souls find salvation. I wanted to go to a remote part of the Ganges, not the clean parts near the Himalayas. I wanted to go to a part near the end, where it was filled with the most prayer and offerings.

Over 600 million people make prayers at the river daily. The prayers first float west and then south to where the river opens into the Bay of Bengal. The water is fertile with prayers there. It is also very dirty. If the most polluted part of the Ganges is still considered holy, then any of us can remember we are holy, too, even on our worst days—even alone in a hotel room.

I go to India with the intention to release his ashes but no plan on how. I fly to Mumbai first, and then I fly to Kolkata, where the river is muddy with dirt and prayers, but flowers still float and grow on it. In Kolkata, I mention to a local tour guide that I want to offer Charlie's ashes to the Ganges. His name is Sujoy, but he tells me to call him Joy. He looks deeply at me as I tell him my story and then says, "After my brother died, my mother became so lost in grief. I will help you." Joy understands my pain. He's going to help me. Out of the 1.3 billion people in India, I somehow chose someone who understood grief. I chose Joy.

Charlie believed in destiny. It was destiny that he met his soulmate Harley in this lifetime. It was destiny that they created two incredible girls, Sunny and Ray. Maybe it was his destiny to die now, but it's hard to think it was his destiny to die alone. Two months before he died, he said to me, "Someday, you'll write my story." He was telling me that it's my destiny to do something with it.

Joy is the local tour guide on a riverboat, the Ganges Voyager II, that I board for a week. We start in Kolkata and then head north on the Ganges towards the Himalayas where many years ago Charlie and I visited. The boat is filled with couples taking once-in-a-lifetime cruises on the Ganges River and with me, a mother sharing a room with her dead son's ashes.

During the week, I don't tell any of the thirty guests of my intentions. During the week, the crew of thirty begins to learn about my mission. On day three of the river cruise, Vishal, the tour manager of the ship, pulls me aside and tells me that in two days, we will do the ceremony. As he speaks, we both have tears.

"Thank you," I say. "Please tell me how much it will be and I will pay in cash."

"I've talked to Partha Mandal, the ship's manager, and there is no fee for this," Vishal says. "We only ask that you donate 500 rupees to the poor."

That is $5. I've budgeted $500 thinking I'd need to buy flowers and water lanterns for the offerings. I ask for 108 offerings (biodegradable lanterns to float in the river) because I want to also include friends and other parents whose children are struggling or died too soon. Vishel and the crew of the Ganges Voyager II tell me they are going to do this for me for free. I'm overwhelmed with the kindness. It's exactly what Charlie and I experienced here when he was young and a family fed us because he was hungry.

Two nights later, the Ganges Voyager II arrives at Mayapura. It's almost 9pm and the skies are dark when I'm invited to join Joy on the support boat our group uses during the day for land excursions. I look around the deck of the small boat and count crew members. In addition to Joy and myself, there are ten of the crew who have been taking care of me all week. Dishel, my room butler. Vishnu, from the spa. Some from housekeeping, from the kitchen, from the dining room...they've all donated their time to help. There are lantern offerings covering every free space on the boat. As I step off the Ganges Voyager II onto the support boat, it feels like I step into the light.

The support boat travels a few hundred feet away from the Ganges Voyager II. There are few lights on the land. The river is as dark as the sky. Joy guides me to the center of the boat to begin a traditional Hindu ceremony. Dishel, who is my son's age, is leading the ceremony. We sit cross leg in front of each other. It almost feels like Charlie is sitting there in front of me. Dishel has become the priest and this small boat has become the temple. Joy and Dishel begin to chant the Sanskrit as Dishel offers a brass container of holy water from the Ganges. It's poured into my hands for me to sip three times. More is poured into my hands for me to touch my head. Then water is sprinkled on me. I follow Joy to the edge of the boat and he gives me an offering with flowers and incense. I kneel down and release it to the river.

"Now the ashes," Joys says.

I open the bag I've carried across the world and put my hand inside as Joy continues to chant. The ashes are soft and fine and flow through my fingers into the river, almost jumping out of the bag, like they are running home to a place they know they are loved, to a place that knows they are holy. I grab another handful and another one. I offer Charlie to the river over and over again. When it's the last of the ashes, Joy leans in to help me and whispers, "Your son shall live in peace now."

On the other side of the boat, the crew begins to release the lanterns one by one as I say prayers and blessings for each person who sent them to me. Over 300 lanterns are offered. I walk to the front of the boat and take photos and videos. I want to record this moment to share with others who supported me during this trip and during the past eight months since Charlie died. But it's too dark for photos and nothing could capture the meaning of this moment for me so I just watched as light after light floats into the river. The Ganges Voyager II is ahead of us and it must be a beautiful sight from the deck to see the lanterns floating by. Joy asks me to follow him and he takes me to the roof of the boat. There is not a place to sit but he motions for me to sit down at the front and then he backs away. I'm all alone at the front edge of the roof and there is light coming from the darkness of the river all around me. Suddenly the sky lights up with fireworks. I look back at Joy and ask, "Are those for…" Before I finish, he nods yes.

As I watch the fireworks, I deeply exhale as my grief meets with grace. The light from the lanterns and the fireworks above illuminates the whole river. It glimmers with hope, it glows love, it shines with Good-Luck Charlie.

GRACE
ON THE GANGES

Tonight, there is a cocktail party before dinner. I put on a dress to cover my grief and walk upstairs to the top deck of the boat. The bar crew greets me smiling, with trays of drinks and appetizers for the guests on the river cruise. The sunset casts a golden glow onto the boat and the water. I still can't believe I'm in India. It's been six months since Charlie died and I've come alone to offer my son's ashes to the Ganges River. Quietly the crew on the boat has helped me to make the arrangements. In three more days, I'll release my son's ashes. In the meantime, I'm a guest on the seven-night river cruise with mainly older couples from the U.S. and U.K. who are here on holiday. No one knows that I'm sharing a room with my dead son's ashes.

I've skipped dinner the past two nights. For six months now, I don't remember how to make casual conversation. I want to avoid questions about the trip and why I'm traveling alone. So far, it's worked. I always choose a chair or table off to the side far from the animated conversations others are having, far from anyone who wants to get close. It's my way to protect myself and it's a way to protect Charlie.

I take a glass of champagne and sit down at the far end of the deck for sunset. Within seconds, a handsome older guest joins me and introduces himself. "I'm Jim," he says. "Are you traveling alone?"

"Yes, I'm alone. I'm Betsy."

"Why did you book the cruise?"

I know he's trying to be friendly and make small talk, but it's a choice for me to tell the truth. I don't like to lie so I choose to tell the truth but not the whole truth.

"I've been here before but not to this part of India," I say. "The river cruise seems like a great way to see parts of India away from the main tourist spots. And I love traveling on rivers."

Jim tells me he and his wife Janet are celebrating their 50th anniversary. Janet joins us and we talk more about work and family, sharing just enough details to keep a conversation flowing. When I find out they are both therapists, it makes me feel safer with them. Then Jim asks how many kids I have. Since Charlie died that question always makes me hesitate.

"I have four children…but now I have three. My youngest son died six months ago."

"I'm sorry," Jim says. "How did he die?"

The question stops me. How did he die? I want to make up a story that he died a hero saving someone from drowning. Or had a tough battle with cancer and our family surrounded him in loving prayers until the end. Those are the types of deaths when people drop off lasagna for the family. When your son dies alone in a hotel room surrounded by drugs, there are no food chains. But even telling him the truth that Charlie died of a drug overdose, doesn't feel like the truth so I don't answer. I smile through the emerging tears and excuse myself. This is why I don't want to let people in. I retreat to my room and skip dinner again.

The next day instead of going with the group tour, I book a private Indian guide for a few hours. He wears a burgundy turban that works well with his handlebar mustache. His name is Raj and like all my guides on previous trips to India, Raj speaks to me like I'm a treasured friend. Raj offers tips on shopping and bargaining. He also sprinkles the conversation with insight on life and spirituality. After two hours with him, I trust him enough that when he asks if I'm married or have children, I share that my son recently died and I've returned to India with his ashes. Raj immediately pulls the car to the side of the road, touches his heart like he feels my pain and asks, "How did he live? What made him happy?"

After six months of people asking me how my son died, I finally found the answer. *Let me tell you how he lived. Let me tell you what made him happy.*

"Charlie loved the water," I say to Raj. "He loved swimming, surfing, and fishing. He loved being on boats especially when he could drive them. Charlie loved hot tubs and long baths. And if he could choose an outfit to wear, it would probably be a bathrobe or a Hawaiian shirt. He was an entrepreneur that loved driving expensive cars. He was also someone who understood when people were hurting, and he quietly offered to help. Charlie loved India; I brought him here when he was eight years old and before he died, he wanted to return. Charlie loved being a father. He has two little girls, Sunny and Ray. On the day his first child Sunny was born, he sent me a text that said, I am so proud of Harley and Sunny. That's what made him happy."

When I finish, Raj bows his head, like I've just offered a prayer. Then he looks at me through the rearview mirror. "I am glad you brought your son back to India."

Later when I join the group on the boat, I see Jim and Janet again. They wave me over and Jim asks, "Would you like to sit with us for dinner?"

The invitation warms me, but I decline.

"I'm going to skip dinner tonight, but please keep asking," I say.

"We're not going to let you get away," Jim says. "We're not going to let you get away."

That feels good to hear. They are meeting my grief with grace. They are giving me space and also letting me know I matter.

DEAR CHARLIE

Dear Charlie,

As I write these words, prayer flags from India are hanging next to me on the porch of my northern California home. There is no wind today, but the second I write your name—*Charlie*—the prayer flags start to flutter, like just the mention of you activates a life force that we all believe is dead. It's a glimmer, a bit of joy, a reminder that the first and last breath you ever took is still living in this world with me, so I take a deep inhale and keep writing.

In January, six months after you died, I wasn't doing well, and someone told me about the "six-month slide," when the impact of grief takes hold just when you think it's getting better. I don't remember what better feels like. I must consciously inhale into my lungs and open my heart to keep it from collapsing inward. It seems like everything in my body forgets how to work. I forget who I was before this grief. I don't know who I am with it.

It was six months after your death when Lisa Marie Presley died. Her death haunted me, because her son died by suicide when he was twenty-seven, the same age as you. She died two and a half years after her son. The news reported Lisa Marie's cause of death as complications from a recent surgery, but as a mother, I know what contributed to her death. I know the constant pain of a shattered heart. I know what it's like to have other children to live for and still be kidnapped by grief.

Six months after Lisa Marie died, Sinead O'Connor's life ended. Her son also died by suicide. He was seventeen. Sinead wrote about trying to live in the months after the death of her son as living as an "undead night creature." I get it. I understand trying to live as undead when part of you feels dead. Sinead lived for eighteen months after her son, and then her life ended too. While I don't personally know them, both these mothers' deaths impacted me because I know the pain and anguish after the shocking and sudden death of a son. It can hardwire the body and mind to wake up in the morning but not want to be awake. I have so much empathy for each day these mothers lived beyond the deaths of their sons—days when you aren't fully alive. Days when you are undead.

I know you wouldn't want me to be in so much pain, Charlie, but it's hard for me knowing you were in so much pain that you needed it to end. You didn't want to be undead anymore either. It's a choice, isn't it? And I have so much compassion for that choice. I'm wanting to get beyond living as undead. My choice is wanting to be fully alive, but often the heartache is so intense that I wonder how my heart can still be beating with the grief holding me hostage.

It's now been a year since I said goodbye to your physical body and opened myself to the possibility of keeping a connection to you as you live in the spirit world. Often, that keeps me between worlds and less present for others. During that year, I always found you in my writing, or maybe you found me. I continue to write to relive every moment of your life, believing that if I could change just one chapter of the story, maybe you would still be here. I'm writing to find you, and I'm writing to find out who I am now.

I joined a grief group with 25,000 other parents who experienced the death of a child. I thought it would help me to know that it gets better, but then one mother wrote it was the twenty-third anniversary of her son dying, and "it doesn't get easier." It was a sobering message. I can't imagine living for twenty-three more years with this crushing ache, and I realize that I am the one who must find the way to escape this world of the undead. I am the one who must discover what makes me feel more alive again.

I start noticing the glimmers of the possibility of the afterlife. The glimmers are the small moments of tiny miracles when it seems like you are waving your magic wand and offering us a rainbow or blessing us with a rain shower. Like when the skies turned cotton-candy pink for your girls, Sunny and Ray, and we all looked up and lifted up our hearts and cheered. There were the hot-air balloons that unexpectedly floated over us in Indiana the night before our celebration of your life. There were the summer months when an orange firefly showed up at the pool every time I was swimming with your girls. The firefly followed the girls as they swam, like it was playing with them. There were the orchids that rebloomed eleven months later on your birthday after I cut the flowers to be cremated with you. There was the river that sparkled with light as I released your ashes in the darkness of the night.

Today as I'm finishing this book, there is a humming-bird at the window. There are no flowers nearby and I'm curious why it flutters its wings at my eye level. It tilts its head and looks at me until I smile—and then it flies away. That hummingbird brings grace to me on a day when I'm writing about your death. You always tried to leave everyone with a smile, and that happened for me again today. Thank you.

Maybe those magical moments have nothing to do with you. Or maybe your death finally made me notice a world that exists for the undead, like there is an unseen world that becomes accessible when someone you love dies. In those glimmers, I believe there is an afterlife for you. The glimmers also show me there is an afterlife for me here in the physical world. On the days when grief consumes me, there is always an invitation to ask for the glimmers and to look for the grace and love that remains. And in those moments, I find you again—and I also find myself.

Love from Mom

WRITING UNDER THE INFLUENCE

WRITING UNDER THE INFLUENCE

At every moment, we are living under the influence of something. It may be grieving the death of a loved one and it can also be living under the influence of falling in love, or holding a newborn baby, seeing a rainbow, watching the sunset. We can be living under the influence of something painful that someone said to us or the influence of praise that makes us feel seen and valued.

Writing under the influence is choosing to take whatever happens to you and write about it to find meaning, healing, and hope. You write to honor the ones you lost, and you write to honor the pieces of yourself that may have been lost or diminished: your body, your worth, your intuition, your faith, your voice.

You write to know the feeling of being held by a loved one so you can remember that feeling when you are lonely.

You write to know the strength of your heart so you can remember that it will keep beating on the days you feel weak.

You write to know and honor pain so that it's witnessed and released instead of hiding in your shadow.

You write to remember, and as you write, you discover the roadmap back to yourself, and you pick up the lost pieces along the way until you feel whole again.

In the weeks after Charlie died, I frequently got lost driving to places I knew. There were also places I had to drive to do things I never imagined doing: to a mortuary, to a viewing, to the coroner's office, to a hotel room to pick up his things. I don't remember the drive home from those places. I was driving under the influence of grief and shock. Writing about those experiences helped me get unlost. It helped me to find my way home to who I was after the death of my son. Writing helped to guide me forward with a tender heart, instead of staying stuck in the heaviness of grief. Writing guided me to see glimmers of the afterlife. Writing allowed me to find grace in the present life.

What helped me the most after my son died were the stories from people who read my writing and then shared their own. Suddenly, the worst thing that ever happened to me was a place of connection with others. Listening to your stories of grief and resurrection helped me to feel less alone as I navigated mine. We heal in community. We grow in connection.

Why writing prompts?

This section of the book is for you to listen and then tell your story. Listening is a form of receiving. Can you give yourself permission to listen and to receive whatever stories that want to be revealed?

There are fifty-two weeks of writing prompts designed around grief, glimmers, and grace. The invitation is to read a prompt and then write for fifteen minutes. You can write on a laptop or in a journal or on the pages of this book.

You may not claim to be a writer, but we all have a story to share. Writing prompts take the pressure off telling a story. You don't choose what to write, the story chooses you. You don't need to be a good writer; you just need to be a good listener and pay attention to your inner voice.

When given a prompt, you read it and then start writing. For fifteen minutes, it's anything goes. There is no way to do it wrong. You don't worry about punctuation or grammar. There may not be a clear beginning, middle, and end. Writing prompts are a way to bypass the stories in your head so you can explore the untold stories of your heart and listen to the unexpressed stories of your inner voice.

I gave my inner voice a name, Betty. My given name is Betty Jane but I go by Betsy. Whenever I have challenges writing about hard things, I call on Betty to guide me. Betty is a little rebellious, definitely braver than me, and always offers up the right words. Betty makes me a better writer. On the days the writing doesn't come easy, try giving a name to your inner voice and invite them into the storytelling.

You can do the prompts in order for fifty-two weeks, or randomly choose a number and open to the page for that prompt. Don't think about the prompt, just start writing and notice where your awareness guides you. Often the story will take you in another direction from the prompt—follow that path and keep writing and don't stop for 15 minutes.

If you are inspired to write daily, it's powerful to do the same prompt for seven days. You may be surprised by the different stories the same prompt reveals. It's even more powerful to do these with a friend or loved one and then read your stories to each other without any feedback.

Writing prompts are like stretching or shaking—the writing loosens up the stuck energy in your body and spirit. The writing creates movement, especially when you are stuck in grief or sadness. Life experiences and feelings that we want to ignore or dismiss can merge into the energy of the organs, muscles, and cells because the memory—and the energy associated with it—has no place to go. When left unexpressed, it begins to slow you down, and then it may keep you down.

There is a heaviness to suffering and a stickiness to sorrow. The grief and sadness want to be held and witnessed before they can be released. Writing creates meaning and that is the space of healing and growth. The writing will not bring your loved ones back to life, but it may bring you back to life.

Thank you for reading my stories. I hope you share your stories, too.

Tell me more…

1

Tell about holding hands.
Tell about letting go.

2

Tell about a childhood toy.
Tell about your childhood bedroom.

3

Tell about burying something.
Tell about planting something.

4

Tell about taking a breath or holding a breath.

5

Tell about what is in your closet.

6

Tell about a pet that died.

7

Tell about a sound you want to remember
or a sound you want to forget.

8

Tell about something or someone that disappeared.

9

Tell about learning to float.
Tell about something that floats.

10

Tell about taking a wrong turn.
Tell about getting lost.

11

Tell about going home.
Tell about leaving home.

12

Tell about saying goodbye.

13

Tell about a hug or kiss—a first one,
the last one, the next one.

14

Tell about a dark night.
Tell about the morning after.

15

Tell about lighting a candle.
Tell about blowing one out.

16

Tell about taking a walk.
Tell about standing still.

17

Tell about a lighthouse, a compass, or something that helped you navigate.

18

Tell about running away.

19

Tell about what is left behind.

20

Tell about looking away.

21

Tell about someone who was like a
mother or father figure to you.

22

Tell about a childhood vacation.

23

Tell a story about angels or guides or ways you feel
supported by the unseen.

24

Tell about what happens next.

25

Tell about having a crush.
Tell about something that was crushed.

26

Tell about learning something new.

27

Tell about someone who made a difference in your life.

28

Tell about learning to meditate.

29

Tell about crossing a bridge.

30

Tell about looking down or looking up.

31

Tell about waking up.

32

Tell about a photograph.

33

Tell about a smell that brings you peace.

34

Tell about a taste that makes you smile.

35

Tell about someone who has eyes like you.

36

Tell about a teacher.

Tell about a teacher that is not a person.

37

Tell about the space between.

38

Tell about a time it rained.

39

Tell about a favorite place in nature.

40

Tell about what part of someone's story has helped you.
Tell about what part of your story could help others.

41

Tell about a recurring dream.

42

Tell about what you wanted to be when you were a child.
Tell about the last time you played, made art, or sang.

43

Tell about a piece of clothing.

44

Tell about taking a trip.

45

Tell about destiny.

46

Tell about what matters most.

47

Tell about the last birthday.

48

Tell about what you are known for
(or want to be known for).
Tell about your living legacy.

49

Write a thank you letter to someone who is still alive.

50

Write a thank you letter to someone who has died.

51

Tell about what makes you feel more alive.

52

Tell about saving someone.
Tell about saving yourself.

RESOURCES

Here are some valuable resources on healing, compassion, and understanding the impact of trauma and grief. Please add your own to the list.

"My Grandmother's Hands" by Resmaa Mankem

Suzanne Guilette, Writer Intuitive, Suzanne-Guilette.com

"The Ancestors' Garden" by Sandra Sam White

"The Myth of Normal" by Dr. Gabor Maté

"What Happened to You?" by Bruce D. Perry and Oprah Winfrey

Gemini Adams, Trauma Recovery Specialist, geminiadams.com

Melanie Ericksen, Intuitive Healing, melanieericksen.com

Kara Kavensky, Record Scratch with Kara podcast, karakavensky.com

ACKNOWLEDGEMENTS

Thank you Suzie Guilette for being a lighthouse for me over and over again during a very dark time. Thank you for reminding me, the dude abides.

Thank you Amanda Coffin for your clear eyes for proofreading and your gentle heart for witnessing these tender stories before anyone else.

Thank you to Uniworld
and the fantastic crew of the Ganges Voyager II:

Partha Mandal (ship manager)
Vishal Bhaskar (cruise director)
Sujoy 'Joy' Banerjee (local tour guide)

Mahendra, Sunil Kumar, Tapas, Dinesh, Anil kumar, Sagar, Anurag, Tanmoy, Mainak, Sudipto, Prashanta, Buddhadev, Soumen, Pintu, Ripon, Vikram, Ajay, Vishnu

Thank you to everyone who sent me a message during this past year. Thank you for your prayers. Thank you for checking on me. Thank you for sharing your stories. You all brought glimmers and grace into the hardest moments of grief.

Thank you to the writers who joined me for a monthly *Writing Under the Influence* circle in 2022 and 2023. Our eight months together was like a liferaft for me. Your stories saved me, your stories kept me afloat. You are all damn good storytellers. Keep writing and sharing.

I look forward to buying your books and supporting your shows.

Thank you to my bonus son Brighton in Zimbabwe. Even thousands of miles away, your messages were a gentle place to rest my grief.

Thank you to Sam, Lucy, and Willie for supporting my grief even as you managed your own.

Thank you to Harley and Sunny and Rayna.
Thank you to Charlie for bringing you all into my life.

It very much feels like Charlie was a co-writer on this book.

Thank you, Charlie, for taking me on an inner and outer road trip as we wrote this book together.

ABOUT THE AUTHOR

Betsy B. Murphy brings healing, humor, hope, and humanity into her storytelling. She invites you into the challenging moments of being human so you can find the place of connection and compassion for yourself and others. Betsy's books include *Autobiography of an Orgasm* and *Write On: A Daily Writing Practice for Anyone with a Story to Tell.* Her documentaries include *New York in the Fifties*, *Something to Cheer About*, and *Althea & Angela*.

You can find out more about her books, solo shows, and films at betsybmurphy.com.